EARLY CHILDHOOD EDUCATION SERIES
Leslie R. Williams, Editor

(continued)

A Matter of Trust: Connecting Teachers and Learners
in the Early Childhood Classroom
  CAROLLEE HOWES & SHARON RITCHIE

Widening the Circle: Including Children with
Disabilities in Preschool Programs
  SAMUEL L. ODOM, ED.

Children with Special Needs:
Lessons for Early Childhood Professionals
  MARJORIE J. KOSTELNIK, ESTHER ETSUKO ONAGA,
  BARBARA ROHDE, & ALICE PHIPPS WHIREN

Developing Constructivist Early Childhood
Curriculum: Practical Principles and Activities
  RHETA DEVRIES, BETTY ZAN, CAROLYN HILDEBRANDT,
  REBECCA EDMIASTON, & CHRISTINA SALES

Outdoor Play: Teaching Strategies with Young Children
  JANE PERRY

Embracing Identities in Early Childhood Education:
Diversity and Possibilities
  SUSAN GRIESHABER & GAILE S. CANNELLA, EDS.

Bambini: The Italian Approach to Infant/Toddler Care
  LELLA GANDINI & CAROLYN POPE EDWARDS, EDS.

Young Investigators: The Project Approach in the
Early Years
  JUDY HARRIS HELM & LILIAN G. KATZ

Serious Players in the Primary Classroom:
Empowering Children Through Active Learning
Experiences, 2nd Ed.
  SELMA WASSERMANN

Telling a Different Story:
Teaching and Literacy in an Urban Preschool
  CATHERINE WILSON

Young Children Reinvent Arithmetic:
Implications of Piaget's Theory, 2nd Ed.
  CONSTANCE KAMII

Managing Quality in Young Children's Programs:
The Leader's Role
  MARY L. CULKIN, ED.

The Early Childhood Curriculum:
A Review of Current Research, 3rd Ed.
  CAROL SEEFELDT, ED.

Leadership in Early Childhood: The Pathway to
Professionalism, 2nd Ed.
  JILLIAN RODD

Inside a Head Start Center: Developing Policies
from Practice
  DEBORAH CEGLOWSKI

Bringing Reggio Emilia Home: An Innovative
Approach to Early Childhood Education
  LOUISE BOYD CADWELL

Master Players: Learning from Children at Play
  GRETCHEN REYNOLDS & ELIZABETH JONES

Understanding Young Children's Behavior:
A Guide for Early Childhood Professionals
  JILLIAN RODD

Understanding Quantitative and Qualitative Research
in Early Childhood Education
  WILLIAM L. GOODWIN & LAURA D. GOODWIN

Diversity in the Classroom: New Approaches to the
Education of Young Children, 2nd Ed.
  FRANCES E. KENDALL

Developmentally Appropriate Practice in "Real Life"
  CAROL ANNE WIEN

Experimenting with the World
  HARRIET K. CUFFARO

Quality in Family Child Care and Relative Care
  SUSAN KONTOS, CAROLLEE HOWES,
  MARYBETH SHINN, & ELLEN GALINSKY

Using the Supportive Play Model
  MARGARET K. SHERIDAN, GILBERT M. FOLEY,
  & SARA H. RADLINSKI

The Full-Day Kindergarten, 2nd Ed.
  DORIS PRONIN FROMBERG

Assessment Methods for Infants and Toddlers
  DORIS BERGEN

Young Children Continue to Reinvent Arithmetic–3rd
Grade: Implications of Piaget's Theory
  CONSTANCE KAMII WITH SALLY JONES LIVINGSTON

Moral Classrooms, Moral Children
  RHETA DEVRIES & BETTY ZAN

Diversity and Developmentally Appropriate Practices
  BRUCE L. MALLORY & REBECCA S. NEW, EDS.

Changing Teaching, Changing Schools
  FRANCES O'CONNELL RUST

Physical Knowledge in Preschool Education
  CONSTANCE KAMII & RHETA DEVRIES

Ways of Assessing Children and Curriculum
  CELIA GENISHI, ED.

The Play's the Thing
  ELIZABETH JONES & GRETCHEN REYNOLDS

Scenes from Day Care
  ELIZABETH BALLIETT PLATT

Making Friends in School
  PATRICIA G. RAMSEY

The Whole Language Kindergarten
  SHIRLEY RAINES & ROBERT CANADY

Multiple Worlds of Child Writers
  ANNE HAAS DYSON

The Good Preschool Teacher
  WILLIAM AYERS

The Piaget Handbook for Teachers and Parents
  ROSEMARY PETERSON & VICTORIA FELTON-COLLINS

Visions of Childhood
  JOHN CLEVERLEY & D. C. PHILLIPS

Ideas Influencing Early Childhood Education
  EVELYN WEBER

The Joy of Movement in Early Childhood
  SANDRA R. CURTIS

The Early Intervention Guidebook for Families and Professionals

Partnering for Success

Bonnie Keilty

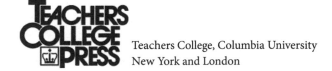

Teachers College, Columbia University
New York and London

*To all the families who opened their doors to me and
shared their thoughts, opinions, values, perceptions,
and everyday lives.*

*To all the professionals and students with whom
I've collaborated and who trusted me as a partner
in their journey of shifting practices and reflective
development.*

Published by Teachers College Press, 1234 Amsterdam Avenue, New York, NY 10027

Copyright © 2010 by Teachers College, Columbia University

Library of Congress Cataloging-in-Publication Data

Keilty, Bonnie.
    The early intervention guidebook for families and professionals : partnering for
success / Bonnie Keilty.
        p. cm. – (Early childhood education series)
    Includes bibliographical references and index.
    ISBN 978-0-8077-5026-1 (pbk. : alk. paper)
    ISBN 978-0-8077-5027-8 (hardcover : alk. paper)
        1. Developmentally disabled children. I. Title.
    RJ135.K45 2010
    649'.1528–dc22   2009020477

ISBN 978-0-8077-5026-1 (paper)
ISBN 978-0-8077-5027-8 (hardcover)

Printed on acid-free paper

Manufactured in the United States of America

17   16   15   14   13   12   11   10   8   7   6   5   4   3   2   1

CONTENTS

INTRODUCTION

There are programs for babies with developmental delays?

Why would your 6-month-old need speech therapy? He doesn't talk yet.

You work with infants and toddlers with disabilities? What do you do, play all day?

These are common questions families and professionals who are involved in early intervention hear. While early intervention for infants and toddlers with or at risk for developmental delays or disabilities is more widely known than in the past, most people are unfamiliar with what early intervention is really about. Confusion is common because the term *early intervention* is used by different types of *helpgivers*. And sometimes, people assume that early intervention happens the same way programs in clinics or classrooms do.

Early intervention can mean many things. For example, the term is used to describe programs that help preschool children who live in poverty get ready for school, elementary age children who have a hard time learn to read, and adults with drug or alcohol dependency end that abuse. In this book, early intervention is a very specific program that is currently available in every U.S. state and territory. Early intervention programs support families with infants and toddlers up to 3 years of age who have developmental delays or disabilities, or who are at risk for developmental delays. Developmental professionals work with families to promote their children's learning and development, as well as meet the needs of their family in general. Early intervention supports are provided by professionals in a variety of disciplines, including early childhood special education, speech language pathology, occupational therapy, and physical therapy.

When one hears the term *physical therapy*, what comes to mind? Perhaps a clinic room full of gym equipment where individuals who are recovering from injury participate in a variety of exercises. A physical therapist, with expertise in the ways muscles work and how the body is positioned, designs and directs these exercises. How about early childhood special education? Maybe one thinks of a classroom full of children participating in a variety of individual or group

1

play activities. The early childhood special educator has expertise in how young children learn and how delays or disabilities impact learning. This teacher creates activities and supports children as they learn during the activities. Professionals such as these, who work in early intervention, use knowledge and skills from their therapeutic and educational backgrounds. *How* the knowledge and practices are used with families with infants and toddlers, however, is different from those typically seen in a clinic or a classroom.

While more people are becoming aware of early intervention for families who have concerns about their children's development, few know what early intervention really is supposed to look like. Professionals are very knowledgeable in their specific area of expertise, and more universities are teaching students about early intervention in general. Professionals, however, might not necessarily have the educational opportunities to understand early intervention specifically.[1] That's where this book comes in. *The Early Intervention Guidebook for Families and Professionals* is intended to answer questions families and professionals have about what early intervention "looks like" when it is based on current research, theories, and policies. *The Early Intervention Guidebook* is written to be a practical, hands-on resource for families and professionals in early intervention. It can be useful for families thinking about or enrolling in early intervention, as well as families already participating in early intervention. Early intervention professionals across disciplines who are new to the field, and seasoned professionals who might not have been trained in early intervention specifically, can use this book. University students across disciplines who are learning about early intervention or completing an early intervention internship will also find this resource useful. In summary, *The Early Intervention Guidebook* is expected to apply research, legislation, practical literature, and recommended practices for families and professionals, and encourage the use of these practices in the everyday world of early intervention.

FOCUS ON FAMILY–PROFESSIONAL PARTNERSHIP

The cornerstone of early intervention is the collaboration between the family and professionals who comprise the intervention partnership. (Note: In this book, the term *family* is used to define those who make up an individual's family as defined by that person. The parent(s) or legal guardian(s) of the infant or toddler with a developmental delay or disability determine who comprises their family. The term *professional* is used to identify any members of the early intervention partnership who are employed to provide early intervention supports.) All members of this partnership bring an expertise critical to early intervention success. The family brings knowledge of their family: their characteristics, what is important to them, what they want for their child, and their child's unique personality. This wisdom is essential to promoting child learning and development for the individual family. Professionals bring knowledge of their own discipline and child development, as well as strategies to support learning, and specifically for children with developmental delays and disabilities. The family–professional partnership blends the general developmental knowledge and strategies brought by the professional and the specific knowledge and experiences of the family to create and implement an individualized plan of action tailored to the family and their child. The success of this partnership and ability to use the expertise brought by each team member depends on both families and professionals having a common understanding of how early intervention works. *The Early Intervention Guidebook* provides this understanding by illustrating early intervention for all members of the family–professional partnership.

EARLY INTERVENTION KNOWLEDGE BASE

What we know about early intervention practice comes from a variety of professional fields. The disciplines of early childhood education, family studies, and developmental psychology bring an understanding of infant and toddler development, and how families work. The fields of special education, nursing, medicine, and allied health (such as speech pathology, occupational therapy, and physical therapy) bring knowledge and practice unique to children with developmental delays and disabilities and their families. Because all of these fields involve families and young children, there are naturally many similarities. Early intervention is a result of blending the theories and research from these fields, what we know about families and young children in general and families of young children with disabilities specifically. The field of early intervention has grown into its own with a body of research, specific policies, and recommended practices that guide early intervention practice.

Theories guide research. Research helps answer questions such as how do everyday family activities promote toddler learning and development? How can families interact with their infant so the infant learns to communicate? For every question answered through research, there seem to be even more specific research questions still unanswered. Why does one activity promote learning and development for a child in one family and not for another child in a different family? What interaction strategies work best for certain families or infants? These more specific, or *second generation*, questions are still being investigated.[2] But families and professionals cannot wait until all the research questions are answered to help infants and toddlers develop as best as they can, particularly because there are never-ending research questions. Also, there is a lot we do know. So, early intervention services continue to occur using the best information we have, while what we know from research continues to emerge, providing us with more and more knowledge to use in our work.

In order to help guide early intervention practice, general statements about what early intervention should look like are developed. Early intervention leaders and policymakers take what we currently know from research, combine it with agreement among professionals and family members who participate in early intervention, and come up with guidelines for how early intervention should be carried out. The Division for Early Childhood of the Council for Exceptional Children (DEC), an international professional association for early intervention, created recommended practices by combining what we know through research and what is generally agreed to in practice.[3] Allied health professional associations have also created practices for therapists to follow (see Web sites in Appendix B). At the federal level, legislation and regulations under the Individuals with Disabilities Education Act (IDEA)[4] outline the requirements for implementing early intervention. *The Early Intervention Guidebook* will illustrate early intervention concepts and components based on what we currently know from theory, research, recommended practices, and policy.

ABOUT THIS BOOK

The Early Intervention Guidebook is designed to provide information about early intervention. Each chapter represents important concepts of early intervention, child learning and development (Chapter 2); family functioning and priorities (Chapter 3); child participation in everyday family and community life (Chapter 4); early intervention as a support not a substitute (Chapters 5, 6, and 7); coordinating the professionals and programs involved in a family's life (Chapter 8); thinking about what's next after early intervention (Chapter 9); and making early intervention effective for all families (Chapter 10). In these chapters, the specific components of early intervention—evaluation and assessment, program planning, intervention implementation, service coordination, and transition—are discussed as they relate to the concepts presented. Each chapter uses applications and examples to illustrate content. Beginning with Chapter 4, there are three reflection opportunities. The first provides an opportunity for families to think about what they will bring to the partnership. The second provides the same opportunity for professionals. The third is located in Appendix A. For each chapter, there is a checklist that can be used to reflect on whether the major concepts of the chapter are being applied within the reader's family–professional partnership. Faculty and students may also use these in case studies or internship experiences.

Chapters 1 through 3 provide a foundation for understanding early intervention concepts and practices. In Chapter 1, "What Is Early Intervention?" the history, concepts, and components of early intervention are introduced. Chapter 2, "The Child's Way: Everyday Learning and Development," focuses on how children learn. Concepts include looking at the whole child versus distinct developmental domains, the importance of engagement and motivation in learning, and learning in the individual family's everyday activities and culture.[5] Chapter 3, "For the Family, For the Child," describes the importance of supporting the entire family. When the needs of family members or the family as a whole are addressed, the family is then more able to focus on helping their child learn.

Chapters 4 through 8 apply the concepts from Chapters 1 through 3 to early intervention practice. Chapter 4, "The Child, Important People, and Particular Places," describes ways of looking at the child during his or her everyday activities so that a clear picture of the child's learning and development emerges. How people interact with the child and the physical space in which the child is participating are also discussed as important components of child learning and development. Chapter 5, "What and Why, Where and When, Who and How: Planning Early Intervention Supports," focuses on different aspects of early intervention planning, including the frequency and intensity of supports and describing the family–professional partnership members and how they work together. Chapter 6, "A Partnership Learning Together," describes the intervention visit. This chapter focuses on the family learning developmental strategies to encourage child learning, the child learning new skills and competencies, and the professional learning the best ways to support the particular family and child. Chapter 7, "Joining the Community," illustrates the role of the community in promoting child learning and development, and how early intervention can facilitate children's learning in the community. Chapter 8, "Making It All Make Sense," describes how the family–professional partnership can best coordinate the supports in early intervention, as well as supports outside of early intervention. This chapter includes descriptions of specific resources for families of children with disabilities, as well as resources that many families use, regardless of their child's developmental status.

Chapter 9, "Considering Now—and Later," brings together a perspective of learning and development that addresses the current outcomes of early intervention while also setting a positive course for future development. This discussion includes planning for transitions, such as the transition out of early intervention when these services are no longer needed or when the child turns 3 years old.

Chapter 10, "Family–Professional Partnerships Going Forward," concludes *The Early Intervention Guidebook* by encouraging readers to apply the described concepts to their early intervention partnership(s).

In addition to Appendix A described above, Appendices B through F provide readers with references and resources. Appendix B is a list of early intervention acronyms used in the book. Appendix C defines terminology used in the book. Appendix D lists national resources available for families and professionals; Appendix E a bibliography of books, magazines and publishers useful for families; and Appendix F a bibliography of books and journals tailored to professionals.

In closing, it is important to identify what this book does and does not provide families and professionals. *The Early Intervention Guidebook* illustrates the fundamental components of early intervention common to all children, families, and disciplinary professionals. It does not cover discipline-specific intervention strategies or methodologies learned in professional training. It also does not include recommendations for children with specific disabilities, such as programs for children with autism. Instead, it focuses on the essential features of early intervention for all families. In other words, it's about *how* the family–professional partnership uses the knowledge and strategies versus *what* are the actual knowledge and strategies. *The Early Intervention Guidebook* is intended to supply families and early intervention professionals with the understanding necessary to collaborate with each other to be successful in the early intervention partnership.

Chapter 1

WHAT IS EARLY INTERVENTION?

When a baby is born, families rely on many different resources to help them as they help their child grow and develop. New parents speak to and learn from their parents, siblings, cousins, and other extended family members. They ask for advice from friends and neighbors who have already experienced parenthood. Families discuss their child's growth and development with their pediatrician and child care provider (if they use one). They learn about milestones and developmental strategies from books, magazines, and television shows. The Internet is also used to obtain general developmental information, as well as have conversations with others through chat rooms and listservs. But what happens when families begin to suspect that their child might be having trouble meeting expected developmental milestones? What happens when families find out their child has a diagnosis, medical or otherwise, that could result in a delay or disability? Early intervention is a resource for these particular situations when more specialized advice is needed.

EARLY INTERVENTION: A DEFINITION

Early intervention programs are designed for families of infants and toddlers (up to 36 months) with or at risk for developmental delays or disabilities. While each state defines the terms *developmental delay* and *disability* specifically, early intervention is for families whose children's development is different from what is expected for their age. It is also for families whose infant or toddler has certain characteristics that make them at risk for developmental differences. The goal of early intervention is to help families set a positive course for their child's development.

All families help their child learn. This is true whether the child is typically developing or not. Families expect to do this as part of parenting. They think about how they interact with their child and what games to play. They think about how they will help their child learn everyday tasks such as getting dressed and eating, as well as learning more "academic" things such as colors and numbers. For families of young children with developmental delays or disabilities, the assumption is not that families cannot do this. It's quite the contrary. Families can and *do* do this. However, because of their child's developmental delays or disabilities, families might need someone to help them figure out how *best* to do this. That's what early intervention is all about. Early intervention is a support program where families and professionals collaborate. Through this partnership, families can meet their parenting goal of helping their children learn and develop as the family envisioned they would.

With that in mind, let's consider what early intervention should and should not be. Looking up the word *intervention*, synonyms are *interference*, *intrusion*, *involvement*, and *intercession*. What images do the terms *interference* and *intrusion* bring about? Perhaps these words sound forceful or negative? They might sound like the purpose is to replace or change something. Consider the advice givers for all families mentioned above. Is intrusion or interference what was envisioned when they were described? Would a parent take advice from a friend or family member who was forcing his or her ideas on the parent? Probably not. Now what about the words involvement and intercession? Perhaps these words sound more helpful, like a go-between or goal facilitator. Early intervention strives to be the latter and to avoid the former. Early intervention professionals try to be the kind of helpers found in friends, neighbors, extended family and, when done well, other professionals involved in the lives of young children. They provide advice and suggestions. Families can problem solve and brainstorm with them. The purpose of early intervention is not to change or add to what families already want for and do with their children. Instead, the objective of early intervention is to understand what the family envisions for their child as part of their family and community, and help them achieve that vision.

WHO'S ELIGIBLE FOR EARLY INTERVENTION?

If early intervention is designed for families with infants and toddlers who have developmental delays or disabilities, these are the children who are eligible, right? It's logical to say that. But what does a developmental delay or disability look like in infants and toddlers? When is a child just developing at a slower pace, but still within the expected range of development? When is a child's development outside the expected range so that specialized supports are needed? It is difficult to identify definitively when a young child has a developmental delay or disability. Yet that is exactly what has to happen for families to enter early intervention. In general, families are eligible for early intervention when their infant or toddler is identified with 1.) a developmental delay, 2.) an *established condition*, or 3.) risk factors that increase the likelihood of a developmental delay or disability.[1]

The term *developmental delay* can be confusing. A delay could imply that a child's development is behind, but could catch up. For some children, this is true. For other children, while they will continue to grow and develop, their development might always be behind, or look different from, that typically expected of their age. It is difficult to truly know the future course of a child's development, or diagnose a specific disability, because children change and develop so much at this young age. Therefore, the term *developmental delay* is used as a catchall phrase to mean, based on how the child is currently functioning in relation to his or her age, that the child could benefit from focused early intervention supports. This definition is helpful in that children who might not have an identified disability—and many do not at this young age—can still receive supports to set them on a positive course of development. This definition is also tricky because there is little research on when a developmental delay, or what kind of delay, could benefit from early intervention and when early intervention is unnecessary.

Each state-level early intervention program has created its own definition of developmental delay for eligibility purposes. Some states have specific criteria, such as a certain percentage of delay. For example, if a state defines developmental delay as a 25% delay, a 12-month-old child would have to be at least 3 months delayed (25% of 12 months), or functioning like a 9-month-old, to be eligible. Other states have more open definitions. For example, in some states, there is no defined level of delay the child has to have in order to be eligible. The early intervention partnership collaborates to decide whether the child's functioning is indicative of a developmental delay.[2]

Families are also eligible for early intervention when their child "has a diagnosed physical or mental condition that has a high probability of resulting in developmental delay".[3] Children with an *established condition*, such as Down syndrome or autism, are automatically eligible for early intervention whether their development is currently delayed or not. Young children with these diagnoses are most likely to have a delay at some point, and therefore it would be beneficial to start early intervention as soon as possible.

States can also choose to include in their eligibility-definition families with children who have certain risk factors that increase the likelihood of developmental concerns. These risks may be biological or medical, such as being born prematurely, or due to family circumstances, such as teen pregnancy.[4] Once again, states determine whether they will serve children *at risk* and define for themselves what at risk means. Some states list certain risk factors and if a child or the family has one of those risk factors, the child is eligible. Other states require a certain number of risk factors for a child to be eligible. Because each state is so different, readers are encouraged to find out the specific eligibility definitions for their individual state.

EARLY INTERVENTION LEGISLATION: A BRIEF HISTORY

Early intervention programs have been around for a long time. Certain states, local communities, and private programs have provided early intervention to families with infants and toddlers with disabilities long before national attention and federal legislation. Local programs still exist that are not part of the federal program, but continue to provide early intervention supports in their community. In 1986, through advocacy from family and professional organizations, the early intervention program for infants and toddlers birth through age 2 years (up to 36 months), became part of the Education for All Handicapped Children Act, which is now known as the Individuals with Disabilities Education Act, or IDEA.[5] This federal legislation mandated public school supports for preschool and school-age children with disabilities, and early intervention was added as an incentive program. That means the U.S. government provides some funds to help states create and implement early intervention programs. In order to get these funds, states need to meet certain requirements, which are outlined in the legislation and regulations. Legislation is law enacted by Congress. Regulations provide more specifics on how states are expected to meet what's in the law. Early intervention regulations are created by the U.S. Department of Education, the federal agency responsible for the early intervention program. States and U.S. territories are not required to participate in the federal early intervention program, but currently all do. At certain times, early intervention federal legislation and regulations are updated. The early intervention program for infants and toddlers with developmental delays or disabilities is currently Part C of the IDEA law, and is sometimes referred to as the Part C Program.

Federal legislation and regulations provide specific requirements that states have to follow. These requirements, however, have to be fairly general to fit the unique situations of each state, local program, and family. With each renewal of the legislation and related regulations, certain requirements change. These changes result from new research and advocacy for ways to improve early intervention. Families or professionals may find that certain aspects of the IDEA legislation or regulations are not specific enough, or what might sound like a good idea on paper actually does not work very well in real life, or gets in the way of effective early intervention. From its beginning and throughout all the changes, known as amendments in government, the federal early intervention legislation has tried to be based on the best research of the time. Using this research, from the field of early intervention specifically and all the related fields identified in the Introduction (child development, family studies, special education, allied health and medicine), certain concepts and components have been identified. These concepts and components are the foundation of early intervention and applicable to all early intervention programs, whether they participate in IDEA early intervention or not.

SIX CONCEPTS OF EARLY INTERVENTION

There are six concepts, or big picture ideas, that are at the heart of early intervention, guiding how early intervention happens. Here, these six concepts are discussed as an overview before exploring them in depth in the rest of this book.

1. Children learn and develop using their curiosity, active discovery, and genuine excitement in the everyday experiences that occur in their family and community. Infants and toddlers learn throughout their everyday lives. They do not have to go to school to learn. They do not have to have special videos or toys. They learn when they are doing—interacting with the people in their lives and looking at, hearing, and touching the objects in their daily activities. They learn through the excitement of exploring what each day brings. They learn competencies and skills needed to participate in the world, and they learn about the important values and traditions of their family's individual culture, or way of life. Children with disabilities are no different. Yet, for infants and toddlers with disabilities, families may have a harder time figuring out how best to provide these experiences due to their child's unique learning needs. Early intervention is there to develop children's interest and participation in these everyday experiences so they can learn and develop based on what's important to their family. Therefore, the overwhelming majority of early intervention supports occur within the family's home and community, during the routine activities in which the child participates every day.

2. Children are part of a family. The goals, values, and needs of the family are the goals, values, and needs of the child. Families provide their children with learning experiences that promote development.[6] These experiences occur with the family, through their everyday life together. However, when a family is concerned about other aspects of family life—stressors such as money concerns or isolation from friends and family—child development is affected.[7] The opposite is also true. When families feel comfortable with family life, they are more able to focus on their child's development. Not only do family stressors impact the family's ability to provide learning opportunities, but they impact the child in general as a member of the family. When one uses the term *family*, the child is assumed to be part of it.[8] Therefore, early intervention cannot only be about the child and his or her developmental needs. It also has to be about the needs of each individual family member and the family as a whole. Therefore, if the family wants, early intervention professionals are available to assist families in meeting goals for the whole family or individual family members.

3. Children learn through the kinds of interactions they have with others and the objects they have to explore. What children learn depends a lot on the kinds of interactions they have with adults and other children. In general, positive interactions are ones that are enjoyable for everyone, there is a lot of back and forth among those interacting, and everyone understands what each other are trying to say. Learning is also affected by the materials (i.e., toys, utensils, and other objects) and setting (i.e., the layout of the area, furniture, and equipment) of the child's everyday routine activities. The child needs safe opportunities to explore in ways that are developmentally appropriate for the child's age and ability, and slightly challenging for the child to figure out. However, every child is different.

Families have to figure out which interactions, materials, and settings are best for their child based on his or her personality and learning style. This is especially true for children with developmental delays or disabilities. What they need in order to learn may be similar to or quite different from what a typically developing child needs to learn. Early intervention professionals partner with the family to determine whether the environment is best set up for child learning, or if adjustments are needed for the particular child. For example, while for many children rough-and-tumble play might be enjoyable, for certain children this type of play can be very uncomfortable and overwhelming. It's not that the interaction itself is inappropriate or negative. But, for a particular child's temperament and learning characteristics, the interactions might need to be modified so that that child is comfortable to learn. Therefore, the early intervention family–professional partnership can identify ways to better promote development according to the child's unique learning characteristics.

4. Families and communities provide many learning opportunities for young children. Early intervention is a support to families and communities, not a substitute. Families have friends, extended family, and others who support them. These are the people who provide parenting advice, give a shoulder to lean on, and an ear to listen. Families rely on these people for day-to-day needs throughout their lifetimes. Families live in neighborhoods and communities where their children will make friends, grow up, and participate in community activities. This does not have to change just because a child has a developmental delay or disability. Early intervention professionals collaborate with the adults who are a part of the child's everyday life so they feel confident they are doing what's best for the child. Professionals do not have to take over the natural role families and others in the community play to promote child development. They are not a substitute for what's already happening. Instead, they collaborate with the family and the community to understand the best way to help the child learn and then support the family and community as they use those strategies throughout the child's day. Early interventionists coach, consult, and collaborate with families and community members so they are comfortable and confident that they can promote child learning, development, and participation in everyday activities.

5. There are multiple resources available for families, but accessing and keeping them straight will require coordination. There are certain developmental supports available to families through early intervention programs. The "big four" are: 1.) special education (known as *special instruction* in early intervention), 2.) speech-language pathology, 3.) physical therapy, and 4.) occupational therapy. A coordinated effort among these supports is needed so that everyone understands what everyone else is doing and learns from each other. Frequently, families also receive supports outside of early intervention. These supports can include various medical and other health providers, as well as social and financial resources. All these different programs, services, and providers can be overwhelming. Therefore, every family who participates in early intervention has a service coordinator who is knowledgeable about the various community resources available to families. The service coordinator is responsible for assisting the family as they move through the early intervention process and bringing together all the pertinent resources.

   6. *Early intervention is just the beginning. As supports are provided in the present, the future is also considered.* At most, families participate in early intervention for 3 years. This is just the beginning for families, as they will parent their child for a lifetime. After early intervention, on or before the child's third birthday, children may receive preschool special education services, or they may have no specialized supports at all. As children grow and have different experiences, different competencies become important. For example, a baby is not expected to be independent. But even in those first 3 years, families do increase their expectations of child independence. The child might begin to help dress herself, make choices, hold his bottle on his own, or even do little chores around the house. Or, when a child goes to child care, the expectations in the classroom might be different from at home. This will continue throughout the child's life, new expectations result from developmental growth and new experiences. In addition to thinking about the goals and competencies the family wants for their child while in early intervention, professionals and families think about the competencies the child needs immediately after early intervention and later in life, as well as how the new programs need to be ready for the child and his or her unique learning characteristics. Therefore, the family–professional partnership thinks about the present and the future simultaneously.

These six concepts are the foundation for implementing successful early intervention. By now, readers might have noticed the many times families of children without disabilities are mentioned to describe how children learn and families function. This is purposeful because children with developmental delays and disabilities and their families are more similar to those without delays and disabilities than they are different. And frequently, it is assumed that needs of children with disabilities are quite different. Actually, children are children first, and families are families first—and then they have special circumstances. This does not take away from the very real needs and unique circumstances of young children with developmental delays and disabilities and their families. That is why early intervention is available in the first place. Specialized supports for young children with disabilities or delays and their families are needed and effective.[9] But not everything has to change for those supports to work. Research has shown that these specialized strategies do not have to be used separately from everyday life.[10] Families can still have the life they envisioned for their family and child. They can still participate in their community as they wish. Early intervention is there to help them achieve their goals.

SIX COMPONENTS OF EARLY INTERVENTION

Throughout the early intervention process, the six concepts are applied. The supports provided through early intervention result from a process of enrollment, assessment and intervention planning, service coordination, intervention visits, and transition. This process is described below.

> During a well-baby check up, Elizabeth Carmina discussed with her pediatrician her concerns with her son Charlie's development. She noticed that he was not crawling, playing, or reaching and pointing to communicate the way her two older children did when they were Charlie's age. Charlie's doctor understood Elizabeth's concerns and told her about the local early intervention program. He explained that Charlie might not be eligible for services, but either way, specialists could look at and provide advice around Charlie's development.

When a developmental concern or risk is identified, a family member, or someone who is part of the family's life, can contact early intervention. In the above story, if Elizabeth wanted, Charlie's doctor could contact the early intervention program for her. The process of contacting early intervention is different for each state. (Readers are encouraged to find out the specific referral process for their state. Contact information for every early intervention program in U.S. states and territories can be found at www.nectac.org/contact/ptccoord.asp/). This first contact with the early intervention program begins the *referral and eligibility* process. Once referral occurs, the early intervention program will schedule an evaluation to determine whether the family is eligible to enroll or not. The evaluators will want to know the child's previous developmental and medical history, including when certain milestones were met, conditions during pregnancy and birth, and any medical concerns. The child's current health status, including hearing and vision, are also needed to fully understand the child's development. The early intervention evaluators use a variety of ways to understand the child's learning and development in everyday life. The evaluators will ask the family questions, observe the child, and possibly ask the child to do certain tasks. Even if a family is not eligible for early intervention, the evaluators can provide information about the child's development and make recommendations on ways to promote further development. If the family is determined eligible for early intervention and chooses to enroll, a plan for intervention is created.

Jessica, a developmental specialist (the title for special educators in this particular state), and Patrice, a physical therapist, came to the Carmina house to determine whether the family was eligible for early intervention. They came in the morning, a time Elizabeth felt was good for Charlie to learn because they usually just "hang out" then. The professionals asked many questions about Charlie's health and the kinds of things he does when playing and participating in family routines. They also watched Charlie as he played with his older brother and sister and ate lunch with his mother and siblings. The professionals discussed with Elizabeth her thoughts on Charlie's development, and what all this information they were discussing and seeing meant to her. They documented the information on different forms and assessment instruments. Elizabeth and the professionals agreed that Charlie's development appeared delayed. They scheduled a meeting for 2 days later to create an intervention plan.

A *plan* for implementing early intervention is used to identify the outcomes expected to be achieved and the services needed to help meet these outcomes. Before a plan can be made, an *assessment* is conducted to gather information needed to make these decisions. The assessment begins by identifying the family's goals and priorities for their child's learning and development—what they want their child to learn. In addition, the family can choose to identify outcomes for their family that early intervention can help address. The plan also includes the names of the family–professional partnership members and how they will work together (that is, how often they will meet with the family and in what settings). Changes in the plan might occur as the child develops and achieves the outcomes, the family changes their minds and wants to address other outcomes, or the child is not progressing with the current plan and a new plan needs to be developed.

Before meeting to create the plan, Jessica and Patrice visited the family on different occasions. Patrice came in the evening to observe Charlie's learning and development when Joseph Carmina, Charlie's father, was home. Jessica watched the morning routine. During the summer, Charlie's siblings were at camp every other day. It was important to see how this time unfolded when the other children weren't there so the plan could consider both situations. During the planning meeting (which occurred in the evening so Charlie's father could attend), it was decided that the physical therapist, Patrice, would come to the Carmina home twice a week to provide strategies around Charlie walking, playing, and using gestures to communicate. Once a week, Patrice would come during the morning playtime, sometimes when Charlie's siblings were there and sometimes when they were at camp. The other weekly visit would alternate between the after-dinner-and-getting-ready-for-bed routine and going to Saturday morning swim class, two activities in which Charlie's father participated and wanted guidance. Jessica, the developmental specialist, would come with Patrice on home visits whenever necessary to provide another professional eye but would mostly work with Patrice outside of intervention visits. A family outcome was also included in the plan—for Charlie's parents to be able to discuss his developmental delays with their other children and with teachers at the swim class and other community activities. Patrice, who is also the family's service coordinator, would collaborate with Charlie's parents on this outcome during her visits. Charlie's family and Patrice scheduled specific days and times for the next week's visits.

Once the plan is created, it is implemented through *intervention visits*. These visits usually occur in the home, community, or classroom, such as in child care programs. For Charlie's family, most visits happen at home. But every other week, there is an intervention visit in the community, during swimming class. The family and professional collaborate during these intervention visits. They identify strategies that promote participation in everyday activities, which result in learning and development. These strategies have to be ones that, with professional guidance, the family feels comfortable using in between visits when the professional is not there.[11] That way, the child can learn throughout the day and week versus just when the professional is there. The *service coordinator* or another early intervention professional can assist the family with meeting any family outcomes.

During the intervention visits, the Carmina family and Patrice brainstormed ways to help Charlie participate during the morning activities, getting ready for bed, and swimming class. Patrice showed Elizabeth and Charlie's siblings how to encourage Charlie to crawl to and from people and toys. She also helped them understand that Charlie needed time to practice crawling, especially since the older children always wanted to help Charlie. At the pool, Patrice and Joseph saw that what happened at the pool was a natural way to strengthen Charlie's muscles. As Charlie got stronger, new strategies were added to continue building his strength for crawling and eventually walking. The family–professional partnership tried different ways to play with toys and interact with others. When Charlie became an expert explorer of toys—banging, shaking, and throwing them— Jessica, the developmental specialist, came with Patrice on one of the home visits to think through next steps in Charlie's play. For the bedtime routine, communication and interaction were the focus, as there was not enough time to let him crawl to and from routines, and the Carminas didn't want to excite Charlie so that he wouldn't sleep. It was after this bedtime routine that Elizabeth, Joseph, and Patrice would sit down and discuss ways to explain Charlie's developmental delays to others. They outlined what the Carminas have said in the past, what felt right and what didn't go so well, and came up with words and phrases so that they were prepared when children asked or when they wanted to explain it to one of his teachers. As the intervention plan continued to evolve over time, the Carmina family continued to work on their desired outcomes at home, as well as during different experiences in the community.

Transitions, or changes that occur when entering, leaving, or while in early intervention, are planned so the child and family move smoothly into the new experience. Even when families first enter early intervention, a plan is created to consider the vision the family has for their child when he or she turns 3 years old and the family is no longer eligible for early intervention. What will the child be doing? Where will the child be? The family's responses to those questions form the basis for the *transition plan*. The transition plan outlines how the child, family, and community will prepare for leaving early intervention.

Three days before Charlie's third birthday, Patrice and Jessica visited the Carmina house to say goodbye. Even though Charlie had been home for his first 3 years, he was about to attend a local preschool program 5 mornings a week. The Carminas felt that Charlie could benefit from frequently being around children his own age, and learning to be in a group setting. Because of Charlie's continued delays, he will receive preschool special education services in his new classroom, where he is the only child with developmental delays. A physical therapist and special educator from the public school system will come into his classroom twice a week to help his teachers. These school system professionals participated in two intervention visits with Jessica and Patrice to understand the strategies used in early intervention. Applying the skills the family honed around communicating Charlie's development to others, Elizabeth and Joseph discussed with his preschool teachers what Charlie would need to participate in preschool activities, and that they expected the teachers to collaborate with the school system professionals so they could learn the needed strategies. The teachers, and school as a whole, welcomed the opportunity. Since Charlie uses pictures to communicate, they bought a specialized computer program—the same program his family uses at home—to make pictures of classroom activities, areas, and objects so Charlie can communicate at school. Charlie visited the program a couple of times, and even made friends before beginning there. Elizabeth scheduled time to be with Charlie the first 2 weeks he attends school to be a resource to the new professionals collaborating with her. During this final intervention visit, the family and professionals reviewed the plans for the transition to make sure they didn't miss anything. Jessica and Patrice let the Carminas know that they would always be available if needed. With all the preparations made, and the final plan in place, the Carmina family–professional partners celebrated their success.

The early intervention process described above begins with referral and eligibility determination. It progresses through intervention planning, intervention visits, and revisions to the plan, and continues until the family transitions out of early intervention. This process is used to achieve the purpose of early intervention, to optimize child development by creating a partnership between the family and early intervention professionals.

FAMILY–PROFESSIONAL PARTNERSHIP

A positive relationship between the family and professionals is essential to successful early intervention. Each partnership member brings strengths necessary to effectively meet the needs of infants and toddlers with developmental delays or disabilities and their families. Families bring knowledge and information about their own family, what's important to them, and what they want for their children. Each family knows how their family functions and their culture, or their ways of being a family and meeting family goals. They bring cultural traditions and routines, materials, and objects. They know their child's nuances and what the family is already doing to support their child's development. Early intervention professionals provide knowledge of child development and children with disabilities, strategies to promote child development, and resources such as materials and other professionals. The family–professional partnership results in teaming, creativity, and a wealth of ideas to brainstorm ways the child can learn. In order for early intervention to be successful, the knowledge, skills, and resources of every member of the early intervention team—family members, early intervention professionals, and community providers—is needed. The purpose of early intervention is to set the child on a positive course for learning and development. A strong family–professional partnership is essential for meeting this goal.

Chapter 2

THE CHILD'S WAY: EVERYDAY LEARNING AND DEVELOPMENT

Meredith Pierce and her 11-month-old daughter Lauren are strolling in the park. Lauren is sitting up in her stroller, looking at everything along the way. A neighbor with a dog walks toward them. Lauren reaches as if to point to the dog. Meredith says, "I see the dog. It's Jeff and his dog is Pepper. We know them." The dog comes up to Lauren, who startles a little. In a calm voice, Meredith says, "It's okay. Look, you can pet Pepper." Meredith gently pets the dog and says, "Nice doggy." Lauren looks up at her mother, then at the dog, and reaches out and pats the dog. Meredith says, "He's soft." Later, Meredith and Lauren are sitting on a blanket in the park. Meredith is clapping and singing a nursery song her parents used to sing to her. Lauren is laughing and bouncing up and down as if to dance. When the song ends, Lauren looks up at Meredith and begins to bounce up and down. Meredith says, "Oh, you want to hear the song again?" and sings the song to Meredith.

Roberto Cabrera calls his two children to dinner. Five-year-old Miguel takes 18-month-old Franco's two hands, and walks with him to the table. Roberto helps both children settle into their seats and gives Franco his bottle. Franco watches as Roberto and Miguel talk about what they did at work and school. Roberto smiles at Franco and asks what he did with his day. Franco smiles, says "Eh" and laughs. Roberto laughs and says, "Bueno!" Kat Cabrera sets down dinner, and serves the children, asking each of them what they want to eat and how much. Kat scoops pieces of chicken onto a spoon and asks Franco, "Pollo?" Franco reaches toward the spoon and says, "Eh!" Kat says, "Pollo, gracias," as Franco takes the spoon and eats the chicken. She asks Franco, "Mas?" Franco again reaches out to the spoon and says, "Eh!" Kat says, "Mas, gracias." The Cabrera family continues to eat and talk about their day. At the end of dinner, Kat opens the dishwasher and Miguel brings his plate to the dishwasher and puts it in. Roberto helps Franco hold his plate and walk to the dishwasher. Roberto puts Franco's plate in the dishwasher.

The examples above reveal that, in the everyday lives of infants and toddlers, there are many opportunities to explore, participate, and learn about the world around them. In fact, it is exactly through these everyday *routine activities* that young children develop. All young children, whether they are identified with developmental delays or disabilities or not, learn when their world is made up of positive developmental experiences. At the same time, what makes experiences positive are unique for each and every child. Children have different strengths, needs, interests, and temperament, even when they grow up in the same neighborhood or family, or attend the same child care program. The early intervention parent–professional partnership creates positive developmental experiences that are tailored to the unique child and apply them in the individual family's routine activities.

WHAT ARE ROUTINE ACTIVITIES?

In general, children learn by participating in the everyday lives of their family and community—those routine activities that children and their families do during their day. Routine activities that occur in most families' lives are playing, eating, getting dressed, and traveling to places. Other activities occur in some families, but not all. Some of these are still quite common, such as walking the dog. Others might be very unique depending on the family's characteristics, such as visiting grandparents who live downstairs or looking for seashells at the beach. The term *routine activity* may be a little misleading. The things families do are routine since they frequently occur in a family's life, such as every day or a couple of times a week. However, they are not necessarily routine in the sense that they have to happen at a set time or a specific way. The things families do are also not necessarily activities in the sense that they have to be planned or have a clear beginning and end. Some families may see "hanging out at home in the morning" as one of their routine activities. Other families may have a daily schedule planned, with specific activities to be accomplished. And still other families might have a combination of planned and spontaneous times.[1] Routine activities are created by the family and reflect how they live their life. They can be as structured or as flexible as the individual family wants them. Researchers have looked at the routine activities occurring in families' everyday lives, and what children learn within them. These researchers found that young children participate in numerous routine activities that provide many opportunities for learning.[2] Clearly, what happens during a family's day is full of opportunities to learn.

In each family's routine activities, children learn expected infant–toddler developmental competencies, or milestones. Consider the competencies Lauren and Franco are learning during the routine activities described above. Lauren is learning:

- what the words *dog* and *soft* mean;
- to strengthen her core muscles and balance as she sits in her stroller and plays on the blanket; and
- to communicate with her mother by pointing to show her mother things she sees, such as the dog, and by bouncing up and down to ask her mother to repeat the song.

Like Lauren, Franco is learning to:

- communicate with his family as he joins in the dinner conversation with his father and brother and responds with sounds and reaching to say that he wants his spoonful of chicken;
- walk;
- use a spoon to eat; and
- make choices as he decides what he wants to eat.

Not only do children learn developmental skills and competencies in routine activities, but they also learn about their family's values and their individual culture, or the "ways of the family." Lauren's family might feel it is important for Lauren to learn to explore and not be afraid of new experiences, such as petting a familiar dog. Lauren's mother is also teaching Lauren about traditions in their family, such as the nursery song passed down from her parents. An obvious cultural aspect of Franco's family is speaking Spanish, the family's native language. Additionally, perhaps Franco's family believes it is important for children to care for one another, as Miguel helps his brother walk. They also might value responsibility as both boys clear their place at the table, and manners as Kat shows him how to say, "Thank you." The traditions of this family may include having assigned seats for meals, choosing what one does or does not want to eat, and children participating in the dinner conversation. Even when the routine activity is the same for many families, such as dinner time, what children learn is different in each family, because how the activity happens reflects the family's individual culture and traditions.

Routine activities are already existing opportunities for children to learn both developmental competencies and their family's values and culture, learning what is meaningful and important to the individual child and family. This is no different for children with or at risk for developmental delays or disabilities. Routine activities are excellent times to use early intervention strategies for learning. The early intervention team can look at the child's routine activities, and determine how best to promote learning within them. The challenge is, for each individual child, how best to create those opportunities for learning.

HOW DO INFANTS AND TODDLERS LEARN?

Frequently, for children without developmental delays or disabilities, families easily create opportunities for their children to learn within the routine activities of family life. Some research shows that families with children with developmental delays or disabilities also think about and find ways to promote their child's learning in routine activities.[3] Sometimes, however, it can be more difficult for families to figure out exactly how best to help their children learn when there are developmental delays or disabilities. This is how early intervention can help. To do this, families and professionals need to understand what makes routine activities positive learning opportunities. While specific routine activities and learning goals are unique to each family's culture, the important features for learning seem to be quite universal.

Practice, Practice, Practice

Children learn best when they have a lot of opportunities to practice new skills or competencies.[4] Children practice newly learned skills over and over and over again, until that new skill is mastered. When a competency is mastered, the child no longer really thinks about using that skill or competency. It just appears to come naturally. But, in fact, it didn't come naturally at all. It came by practicing many, many times. Consider a child learning about putting objects together. This is called *relational play*. The child might learn how to put objects in and out of a toy bucket. At first, the child might be banging an object on a bucket, and the object falls into the bucket accidentally. The child might watch an older child put objects into a bucket. Then, the child begins to purposely try to put objects in the bucket. Sometimes the child over- or undershoots the bucket, and some of the objects fall outside the bucket. After trying this a few times, the child gets all the objects in the bucket, sometimes on the first try, sometimes after a couple of tries. Once all the objects are in the bucket, the child dumps them out and tries again. A child might do this a lot without getting tired of the game. Over time, the child can easily judge what he needs to do to put the objects in the bucket and quickly drops all the objects in the bucket without missing a single one. The child has mastered the skill of putting objects in a bucket. Routine activities by their very nature provide many and frequent opportunities for learning new competencies.[5] Consider Franco in the opening story. One can assume that his family eats dinner every day. Seven times a week, Franco has opportunities to learn the competencies promoted during dinner time. If the same learning occurs during breakfast and lunch, that's 21 times per week that Franco can practice developing those competencies.[6] More specifically, consider how Franco's mother is promoting communication by showing him how to say the words *gracias* and *mas* so he can imitate them. Say she does this 20 times during the meal. That's 140 times per week during dinner alone that

Franco has an opportunity to learn to use those words! The more opportunities the child has, the more likely the child will learn and master specific developmental competencies.

Competencies are learned best when the opportunities to learn do not just happen in one routine activity, but in different ones, with different people and objects.[7] For example, the child above can learn about relational play by practicing:

- when he cleans up toys by putting them in his toy box,
- during bath time as he pours water into different cups,
- in the backyard as he slides leaves through the slats on a lawn chair, and
- during snack time when he repeatedly takes Cheerios in and out of his bowl.

Not only does this provide even more opportunities to practice, but it also allows the child to learn and use the skills in different situations. This is called *generalization*.[8] While as adults we can take something we've learned and apply it to different situations, young children learn much better when they are learning the competencies in the situations where they are expected to use them.[9] Young children are less apt to generalize newly learned skills to different routine activities, people, and objects. They need to practice these emerging skills with the different people and objects that are a part of the routine activity. Let's return to Franco and learning to imitate words. He can learn to imitate words in other places than mealtimes. At the park, he can imitate "mas" so his father will push him on the swing. He can make choices on the clothes he wants to wear by pointing (or learning to point). He can imitate words when reading books with his brother. And so on and so on. Not only does learning in these routine activities dramatically increase the number of opportunities for practice, but it also takes care of the issue of generalization. Early intervention can help take advantage of these natural opportunities for practice and generalization by supporting families during routine activities. That way, the family, including the child, does not have to figure out how to generalize skills learned in a clinic or made up activities, because they are learning them in the actual activities where they will use them.

Participation Is the Key

In order for routine activities to be opportunities for learning, children need to be actively participating in them.[10] Participation is not sitting on the sidelines watching. It is interacting with objects and others. This is called *engagement*. Sometimes, we don't think about engaging infants and toddlers in routine activities, when in fact there are ways they can participate. For example, in the grocery store, we sometimes think of it only as an errand—buying groceries. For the young child, however, it's an opportunity to see and talk about what's happening, and explore products; basically, to learn. Even young infants can touch and look at different products while shopping. Just talking about what the parent and child are doing or what's going on around them promotes development. Older infants can choose between two products, and hold them. Toddlers can name products and place products in the shopping cart. Older toddlers can match products and coupons, and talk to the grocery store staff. Diaper changing is another time when families don't always think about engaging their child. Children can be spoken to about what's going on, they can move their legs when asked and hold the diaper. Older toddlers can get the diaper when asked and pull their pants up and down. How a child engages in routine activities is individualized based on the child's age and abilities.[11]

For children with developmental delays or disabilities, engagement might not come easily. Children with developmental delays or disabilities have been found to be less engaged than children without disabilities.[12] Sometimes, families may not be sure how their child can participate. For example, Franco's parents may not think about including him in the dinnertime conversation because he doesn't really talk. But instead, his parents have found a way to make sure he does participate in this family time. Early intervention professionals can collaborate with families to determine ways children can participate in the routine activities. That way, new competencies are learned and mastered.

The "Just Right" Challenge

As one competency is mastered, children need the opportunity to learn new, more challenging ones.[13] Families naturally do this for young children, and children naturally look for these opportunities. As an infant masters crawling, family members encourage the infant to stand and then learn to walk. As a toddler masters using one word to communicate, family members encourage him to put two or three words together. For Franco, a next step toward walking might be to have only one hand held rather than two hands, or to walk using a push toy rather than with his brother helping him. Or to communicate, his mother might ask him to sound out the first letter of the words she's saying, instead of accepting any sound as his way of communicating to her. Family members usually take their cues from their child. Infants and toddlers usually want to learn new competencies as they master old challenges.[14] They begin to look for new challenges. This behavior is usually interpreted by families as the child being bored or tired of his or her old toys, games, and so forth.[15] As family members see their child looking bored, they up the ante of what's expected of the child. When an infant is no longer interested in rattles, toys to chew on, or banging objects together, an adult provides new toys that can be stacked, put together, or dropped into. Creating the just right challenge can happen by setting new expectations for the child to interact with objects and others. This could include:

- providing new materials or objects for the child to explore, use, and learn from;
- providing new experiences with adults or children;
- showing new ways to explore, use, and learn about materials and objects the child already has; and
- showing new ways to interact with adults and children the child already knows.

The challenge for all families and professionals is determining that "just right" challenge for the individual child. Early intervention professionals can collaborate with family members to determine what next step would be just enough of a challenge for their child. The new competency should be just slightly more difficult than what the child already knows how to do.[16] If it's not, then it's too easy, and the child would not be learning anything new. At the same time, the next step should not be so hard that the child does not understand it or, at this point in the child's development, would be impossible for the child to learn.[17] The risk in creating challenges that are too hard is that the child might begin to think that he or she cannot learn at all or make things happen in the world.[18] Then, the child might be less willing to try. If Franco's mother asked him to make the first sound in the word, that might be just enough of a challenge. But expecting him to say the whole word at this point is most likely too hard. If no one responded to Franco trying to communicate by just making the first sound because they're waiting for him to say the whole word, he might think no one understands him and stop trying. So it's tricky to get the "just right" challenge just right. Early intervention professionals and families can determine the just right challenge for their particular child within specific routine activities.

The Unique Strengths of Each Child

Just as families and professionals bring strengths to the early intervention partnership, each child brings his or her unique strengths, which provide important clues on how best to promote learning. These strengths include the child's interests, current competencies, and temperament.

Think about what, as an adult, personally interests you. Now think about certain things that do not interest you at all. From those two lists, which would grab your attention? Which would you want to learn more about? Odds are, the list of interests is what you would want to spend your time doing and learning about. Now consider times you had to participate in or learn about topics that did not interest you. Think about how hard it was to *pay attention* and really *understand* the material. Think about how hard it was to *use* the material learned. Young children are the same way. Each child has their own unique interests—those things that grab their attention, ways they want to explore, and new ways they want to try out things.

Each child also has things that do not interest him or her. Unlike adults however, young children do not understand what adults have learned over time—sometimes people need to learn things even if those things are not interesting to them. Infants and toddlers simply won't participate in activities that are not interesting to them. Therefore, learning occurs best when adults either build on what the child is already interested in, or create new interests for the child.[19] For example, Lauren showed she was interested in the approaching dog by looking at and pointing to the dog. If she didn't do this, Lauren's mother might have tried to build interest, perhaps by pointing at the dog to see if Lauren became interested in it. If Lauren protested or showed great fear of the dog, then Lauren would be communicating that she was not interested and it would be best for her mother not to force her.

Sometimes, however, children need to participate in routine activities that they do show disinterest in or even protest about. For example, a child may have no interest in getting in the car seat, a requirement to travel anywhere. When this occurs, the family and professional could first determine if there are any developmental reasons the child might not want to get in the car. For example, the child might associate the car with doctor appointments. This situation is not only uninteresting to the child, but potentially negative. Or, the family–professional partnership might figure out the child becomes overwhelmed with all the sights and sounds that occur while riding in the car. These reasons would require different strategies. But, if it is determined that riding in the car is simply not interesting to the child, the family–professional partners could identify ways to make it more interesting. For example, if a child enjoys music, the parent might put on a child's CD, or sing to the child while driving. Or, if a child likes to look at books, there could be one or two books that are only available to look at in the car. Of course, children's interests change, so adults always need to be on the lookout for new ways to interest the child. Once interest is built into the routine activity, the child is then ready to learn.

Another strength the child brings to learning is his or her current developmental competencies. As parents witness every day, children are born ready to learn, with certain competencies in place so they can learn new competencies. Children continue to develop new competencies by building on what they already know how to do. For instance, a typically developing infant focuses on her mother when she speaks and smiles. The infant then begins to respond to and initiate interaction with smiles and sounds. This back and forth then turns into back and forth with syllables (ba-ba-ba) and play, with both parent and child taking turns banging objects together. This turn-taking then evolves into more complex back and forth conversations and imitation of ways to solve problems and use objects. This same process occurs for children with developmental delays and disabilities, with some modifications. Children learn best when adults build on what the child already knows how to do.

How a child learns also depends on his or her temperament, or personality. Temperament includes:

- how a child adapts to changes in his or her everyday life and reacts to new situations;
- the level of intensity with which a child responds to sights, sounds, and movement;
- the predictability of a child's rhythms or schedule; and
- a child's attention to and persistence in participating in everyday activities.[20]

Usually, a child is considered to have temperament strengths when the child reacts to the world, but in a controlled way:

- When a child is in a *new situation*, he doesn't avoid it, nor does he run right into it without any concern. Instead, he slowly tests it out.
- A child does not ignore or overreact to *sights and sounds*. Instead, he is aware of them and responds with restraint.
- A child is on a *predictable schedule*, but also can deal with changes to that schedule.
- A child will *continue to try* despite limited success, but doesn't give up after one try or obsessively try much longer than is useful.

While these traits are considered temperamental strengths in general, any temperamental characteristic can be a strength depending on how adults understand and use them. Here are two examples about persistence. In one situation, a child is persistently trying to scoop his snack with a spoon. In another situation, a child tries once to scoop his snack but is unsuccessful. He puts his spoon down and eats with his hands. The parent of the first child may provide encouragement by describing how much the child is working on eating with a spoon. The parent is supportive and available in case help is needed, but leaves the child to continue to figure it out (practice) on his own. The parent of the second child might be more involved in helping the child try. The parent might show the child how to put the food on the spoon with his fingers (already a competency) and bring the spoon to his mouth. This parent helps the child be successful with the spoon so the child keeps trying. In both examples, each child's temperament is a strength because the parent responded to the child's temperament characteristics in a positive way. Therefore, understanding a child's temperament, as well as the other areas of interest and developmental competencies, are strengths when adults understand and use them to create positive learning opportunities.

Responsive Adults

How family members interact with their children impacts how and what children learn.[21] These interactions can be positive or negative. Positive interactions that promote child development are called *responsive interactions*. Responsive interactions occur when an adult understands a child's signals or cues and answers the child, or responds according to what the child is trying to say. Meredith Pierce and the Cabreras used responsive interactions. There are four aspects of responsive interactions:

Sensitivity: Families are attuned to the child's individual characteristics, such as interests, competencies, and temperament, and can accurately read their child's communication and respond by providing what the child needs.

For example: The child is shaking his or her head "no," and the caregiver responds by removing the unwanted object or ending the behavior. Or, family members understand the different cries of a young infant and provide what the child needs for each cry.

Children learn: They are safe in the world, there are people who will take care of them, and their communication is understood.

Contingent Responsiveness: The way a family member interacts with the child is dependent, or contingent, on what the child does first.

For example: Both of Franco's parents contingently responded to his interactions. They both waited for him to vocalize before responding. When Franco said, "Eh!" in response to his father asking about his day, Roberto responded positively that Franco was contributing to the conversation. When Franco reached for the spoon and vocalized "Eh," his mother responded by giving him chicken.

Children learn: They can have an effect on their world and can make things happen. They also learn they have to do something, and usually something specific, in order to make a something else happen.

Consistent Responsiveness: Family members respond to the child's specific behavior the *same way, every time* the behavior occurs. Young children like it when their world is predictable.

For example: Family members always respond to the infant's cry.

Children learn: They can anticipate what's going to happen next; they know what to expect. They can count on family members and independently explore, learn, and try new behaviors in the safety of their family.

Engagement: The different ways families help children actively participate in routine activities. General ways to promote engagement are:
  • Watching the child's behaviors to decide when to step in and when to wait and see what the child does on his or her own.
  • Being available to help the child learn as needed, such as showing

the child ways to engage, commenting on what the child is doing, or responding when the child asks for help.

- Following the child's lead when interacting and playing.

These responsive interactions can be hard for families of children with developmental delays or disabilities. Frequently, these children's signals are different from, or more subtle than, how typically developing children communicate.[22] The family–professional partnership can work together to identify how the child is communicating and what the child is trying to say.

The specific ways families promote their child's learning will depend on what's important to the individual family culture and the unique learning characteristics of the child. The family–professional partnership can only determine that. How adults interact with their children, however, has been found to be related to children's future learning and development.[23] Therefore, many early intervention research projects have used parent–child interaction as the basis for promoting child development.[24]

In summary, children learn best when they can:

- practice new competencies over and over again in different routine activities and with different people and objects;
- actively participate in routine activities;
- figure out a just right challenge;
- use their unique strengths; and
- rely on responsive family members to learn and develop.

These characteristics may seem overwhelming in a list like this. It is hoped, however, that none of them seemed out of the ordinary when they were described. These are the many ways young children learn that early intervention professionals know about and bring to the partnership. Families come to the partnership knowing what they look like in their particular family. Together, the early intervention partnership can determine how best to make sure the child's everyday life is full of ways to promote child learning and development. That way, the infant or toddler can learn the expected competencies or tasks of early childhood.

WHAT DO INFANTS AND TODDLERS LEARN?

Every family will decide what they want their infant or toddler to learn while participating in early intervention. The goals families have for their children will depend on the family's individual culture and developmental expectations. In Franco's family, he is expected to help clear the table, but he also still uses a bottle. For other families, they might expect a child Franco's age to be off the bottle, but not yet helping with "chores." What one family expects a child to do at a certain age, another family might not expect until a later age. For example, researchers found that Anglo families expect their child to use utensils at about 18 months, Puerto Rican families expect this skill at about 27 months, and Filipino families expect this skill at about 32 months.[25] They also found that Anglo mothers tended to want their children to have a positive sense of self, but also be kind and caring. Puerto Rican families tended to focus on their children having a sense of decency and a demeanor of respect, and be accepted by the community. Therefore, ethnicity might play a role in determining what developmental competencies families want their child to achieve as well as when they expect their child to achieve them.

Other family characteristics also determine what children are expected to learn. In urban areas, children are going to have opportunities to learn about crossing streets and taking public transportation. In suburban and rural areas, riding in cars is more likely. The specifics of what children learn and what development looks like depends on the individual family. But there are certain developmental "tasks" of infancy and toddlerhood.[26] These competencies are broadly discussed below.

Developmental and Functional Competencies: Multiple Ways of Participating

Many infant development books for new parents and emerging professionals divide young children's development into different domains. These domains are:

Cognitive: Thinking, such as problem solving, and learning concepts such as colors, size, and shapes.

Communication: Expressing oneself through words, gestures, and body language, as well as understanding what others are trying to express.

Motor: Is divided into gross motor and fine motor:

Gross motor—Using arms and legs, such as reaching, throwing, crawling, walking, or running.

Fine motor—Using the smaller muscles in the hands and mouth, such as grasping objects, scribbling, using mealtime utensils, and chewing.

Social-emotional: Feelings and interacting with others.

Adaptive: Self-help skills for everyday needs, such as bathing, toileting, dressing, and safety.

Within these domains, specific skills or milestones are identified, along with certain ages in which those milestones usually develop. While this method provides a simple way to look at development, actual development is more complex. In reality, children use all these domains together to *function*, or participate in a routine activity.

Take walking as an example. Walking is usually considered a gross motor competency. It does indeed require gross motor skills such as balance, coordination, and muscle strength. But learning to walk also requires having a reason to walk, problem solving how to get up and walk, and figuring out that walking is more efficient than crawling. These skills are considered *cognitive competencies*. In addition, the child needs to feel secure enough to leave the safety of staying near one's family members to venture out and explore on one's own. This is considered a *social-emotional competency*. Therefore, learning to walk requires more than just gross motor skills.

Walking by itself is not really a routine activity. Routine activities are even more complicated in terms of the competencies needed to participate. Trying to fit child participation into one domain becomes impossible as children use competencies across domains to function in routine activities. Returning to the initial examples in this chapter, below is a list of all the skills Lauren and Franco are learning while participating in their routine activities.

Lauren's Learning Competencies:

Sitting and balancing
Watching
Understanding words
Pointing to communicate "What's that?" or "Look at that!"
Using her body to communicate "Do it again!"
Controlling her fear
Confidence in petting the dog
Imitating petting
Learning words of the nursery song
Balancing her body while bouncing
Enjoying interactions with her mother
Communicating enjoyment through laughing
Moving to music

Franco's Learning Competencies:

Walking with two hands held, which includes balancing and coordinating
Responding to questions
Taking turns in conversation
Being social with his family
Holding a spoon
Making choices of how much food he wants
Asking for "more"
Walking while holding an object
Completing tasks such as clearing his place

And these competencies are just from a few short sentences in the examples. Imagine how many developmental competencies each child actually is learning in one day with the multiple routine activities that occur. To help children learn as they participate in routine activities, the early intervention partnership thinks across developmental domains so that all areas of development are being promoted.[27]

For children with developmental delays or disabilities, the way children meet everyday goals might look different from what is usually expected. For example, a child who has trouble speaking words but is good at manipulating with his hands can learn gestures and sign language to communicate. The child is still communicating. He is just using signs instead of talking. A child who has difficulty crawling but has mastered rolling over can use rolling as a way to move around to play and interact. The child is still moving on his own to get to different places. He is just using rolling instead of crawling. The *function* is still the same—communicating and moving around—just the *form* for doing it is different.[28] Of course, any alternative forms, if needed, have to be acceptable to the family. The family–professional partnership collaborates to determine the best form to help the child participate in the routine activities.

Independence or "I Can Do It!"

One aspect of engaging in routine activities is what the child can do by him or herself, or independently. Again, independence is influenced by many things, like the child's age and family's culture and expectations. In general, even typically developing infants and toddlers do not necessarily do a lot of activities fully independently. There are, however, some activities that children can do completely by themselves for short periods of time, such as playing, drinking from a bottle, or eating with his or her fingers. For other routine activities, the child might do part of the activity independently. For example, Franco did not scoop food onto his spoon, but he did bring the spoon to his mouth to eat. Early intervention can help families promote their child's independence in areas the family wants and as much as the family feels is appropriate.

There are two ways children can become independent. Independence can come with learning new developmental competencies. As the child ages and becomes more competent, the child has more ability for independence. For example, a young child might be able to slide her feet into her shoes, but her father ties them for her. Not until she is older and has more coordination in her fingers can she tie her shoes, and therefore independently complete the activity of putting on her shoes. The other way children can become more independent is by changing the activity in some way to make it suitable to their abilities.[29] Using the same example, if the child had Velcro shoes, she could most likely put on her shoes by herself much earlier than if she had to tie them. There are many examples of ways adults make it easier for infants and toddlers to become independent. For young infants, there are rattles with Velcro to attach to wrists or ankles for the infant to independently shake the rattle without having to grasp it. Blow-up ring seats provide support for infants when they have the head and trunk control to sit, but not the balance. Cups with lids allow toddlers without the coordination to avoid spills to drink from cups.

Creating independence with materials can also be used for children with disabilities.[30] For example, Franco can become more independent by not having to rely on a family member to help him walk if he had a push toy he could use while walking. This, of course, would have to make sense within the family's culture. For example, maybe the family wants family members like Miguel to help Franco. Another example could be that Franco has a machine that "talks" for him when he presses a button to ask for "more" or to make choices, such as what he wants to eat or choosing someone to help him walk. By finding different ways for the child with developmental delays or disabilities to learn new competencies, he or she can also be learning independence, and with that a sense of accomplishment and positive self-concept.

With the family's knowledge of what they want their child to be more independent in doing and the early intervention professional's knowledge of strategies to increase independence, the intervention partnership can determine the best way to promote the child's independence in specific routine activities.

Interacting with Others

From the first moments after birth, young children are learning by interacting with others, and learning to interact with others. When infants and toddlers interact with those who know things they do not, they have different experiences and learn different competencies than they would by themselves.[31] In the opening stories, Lauren and Franco are learning by interacting with their families. Lauren is only learning the nursery song of her family and feeling comfortable enough to touch the dog because she is interacting with her mother. Franco is learning new words and experiencing walking because he is interacting with his family. By interacting with others, infants and toddlers learn about things they could not figure out on their own.

Infants and toddlers are also learning *how* to interact with others. They learn to take turns in conversation. They learn to get and keep another person's attention. They learn how to express one's thoughts. They learn effective ways to communicate with others, like Lauren and Franco did. Interacting with other children of the same age can be challenging for young children. They have to share objects and play space. They have to figure out how to play with each other when each play partner might have a different idea of what they should be doing. There are a lot of very difficult concepts for young children to figure out, and toddlers are only beginning to do this. They need to figure out how to cope with others while they are still figuring out how to cope with their own needs and the physical world around them.

Regulating Oneself

Lauren Pierce was born 4 months premature. As is common for infants born this early, she sometimes has a hard time coping with the world around her and needs her mother, Meredith, to help manage it. Lauren used to need to be wrapped snugly in a blanket and rocked to sleep for naps and bedtime. Now, for naps, Meredith can put Lauren in her crib and pat her back and talk softly to her until she falls asleep. At night, she still needs to be rocked to sleep with the blanket, although not so snugly wrapped. Lauren also used to get very stressed by loud noises and any unexpected changes. When something startled, excited, or scared her, she would become very overwhelmed and cry. It would take a lot of consoling for Meredith to calm her. Meredith was impressed when Lauren was surprised by the dog but reassured by her mother's voice and showing her the dog was nice. Meredith feels confident that Lauren will become more and more able to cope as she gets older.

Being able to regulate oneself is the foundation for all other learning.[32] Regulation occurs by coping with sensations or changes in one's environment, known as *stressors*. These stressors can be happening internally to the child, such as being hungry or tired. These stressors can come from outside the child, such as loud noises, meeting strangers, or overstimulating environments. Children learn to regulate their rhythms, such as anticipating routines, coping with changes to their schedule, and going from awake to asleep and asleep to awake. Children are also learning to regulate their emotions, including the strength of their emotions and how long the emotion lasts. As toddlers, they are just beginning to learn to wait, organize, attend, and follow the rules of others. These tasks are all somewhat challenging for children. For those with developmental delays and disabilities, they can be even harder to achieve. Learning to cope with the world comes gradually for all children.

As adults, we have learned how to deal with many stressors. Infants and toddlers are just beginning to learn this skill and require the assistance of adults to cope. How much and what they are expected to cope with depends on the individual family and their beliefs.[33] For example, some families expect children to be put in a crib awake and go to sleep on their own. Other families will rock children to sleep. It will also depend on the needs of the child. Meredith Pierce might have wanted to have her child fall asleep on her own. But Lauren's developmental characteristics resulted in Meredith providing more support because that's what Lauren needed.

The infant–toddler period is the beginning of "the gradual transition from extreme dependence on others to manage the world for us to acquiring the competencies needed to manage the world for oneself."[34] As children grow older, they are expected to cope with more stressors themselves. For example, if an infant becomes startled by a loud noise, her parent might comfort her by physically hugging her. If an almost-3-year-old startles, the parent might provide verbal comfort by telling her she's okay and explaining what the sound was so the child can regulate her own emotions. As the child demonstrates that she can handle more, the family slowly gives more of the coping responsibility to the child. When the child is regulated, he or she is ready to explore and learn.

These different tasks of infancy and toddlerhood are general areas of early development. The specific tasks, or goals, for a child depend on the family. What does the family think is important for the child to learn? How does the family want the child to participate more in their routine activities? What does the family want their child to be able to do when he's 3 years old, entering kindergarten, or as an adult? These questions will guide the individual goals for early intervention.

THE BIG PICTURE: RELATED POLICIES AND GUIDELINES

The concepts described in this chapter's previous sections are based on theory and research. They are reflected in early intervention policies and recommended practices. These guidelines help families and professionals design early intervention programs attuned to the multiple learning opportunities available in routine activities, and the unique development of each young child within his or her family culture.

The importance of learning in routine activities is clear in the Individuals with Disabilities Education Act (IDEA) legislation and regulations, as well as recommended practices. IDEA states that early intervention services "to the maximum extent appropriate, are provided in natural environments, including the home, and community settings in which children without disabilities participate."[35] This expectation of using "natural environments" for early intervention visits has been in the early intervention legislation since it was created in 1986. In 1997, the federal government added stricter language by requiring that early intervention be provided in non-natural environments *only* "when early intervention cannot be satisfactorily achieved for the infant or toddler in a natural environment."[36] This is determined by the family's early intervention team, which of course includes the family. Based on current early intervention research, developmental psychologist Carl Dunst and colleagues further defined the term natural environments by stating that "natural learning environments are not places, but rather the experiences afforded children in the context of activity settings that make up the fabric of family and community life."[37] In other words, early intervention best supports child learning and development by promoting the child's active participation in his or her everyday routine activities so the child learns functional competencies within the culture of his or her own family.

Individualized, integrated development is also in early intervention legislation. IDEA uses words such as *child functioning* and child's *strengths and needs* in child assessment.[38] And while the child's present level of development in each domain is needed for the intervention plan, the expected outcomes for children participating in early intervention are actually integrated and functional. The Early Childhood Outcomes (ECO) Center is funded by the Office of Special Education Programs (OSEP) at the U.S. Department of Education to identify general outcomes for all children and families who participate in early intervention (see www.fpg.unc.edu/~ECO/index.cfm/). The ECO Center identified three child outcomes. Infants and young children will "demonstrate improved: 1.) Positive socio-emotional skills (including social relationships); 2.) Acquisition and use of knowledge and skills (including early language/communication); . . . [and] 3.) Use of appropriate behaviors to meet needs."[39] These outcomes were purposely designed to be functional rather than developmental domains.

In addition to the ECO Center outcomes, many states are designing early learning guidelines that are used to determine how effective programs are in promoting learning for all children. These guidelines are unique for each state. For specific state-level information, readers are encouraged to explore their state's early learning guidelines. Because more and more states are using early learning guidelines, national early childhood associations (National Association for the Education of Young Children and the National Association of Early Childhood Specialists in State Departments of Education) felt they needed to advise states on how early learning guidelines can be helpful to local early childhood programs.[40] Three criteria are that early learning guidelines must be:

- developmentally appropriate for young children and how they learn, considering children's diversity, including their culture, language, experiences, and abilities;
- based on research and the views of various constituents, including families and practicing professionals; and
- assessed through strategies that make sense for young children, including ones that are individualized, interest-based, and considerate of children's abilities, culture, and experiences.

When early learning guidelines make sense based on what we know about young children's development, they can help early intervention professionals and families make decisions about what their individual child can and should learn within his or her everyday experiences.

SUMMARY: THE CHILD'S WAY

All children, with and without developmental delays and disabilities, need the same things to learn and develop. Children learn by actively participating in the everyday life of their family by interacting with others and meeting just right challenges. It is within these routine activities that infants and toddlers practice and generalize their new abilities. These abilities, while unique for each family and child, include integrated, functional competencies, independence, interaction skills, and regulation. Families and professionals in early intervention collaborate to identify the developmental abilities important for their individual child, and create learning opportunities attuned to the child's learning characteristics so the child can develop along a positive path.

Chapter 3

FOR THE FAMILY, FOR THE CHILD

Sean Crause and Jolie Simmons moved to a large west coast city for Jolie's dream job. At about that time, they found out they were having twins. It's been a year since the birth of their sons, Elliot and Aiden. For the first year after the boys' birth, friends and family from the couple's hometowns were constantly visiting to help out. Now, Sean and Jolie feel like they are finally settled into a routine as a family of four. Elliot's seizures are pretty much under control and both parents are back at work. The boys attend the child care center at Jolie's corporation. Their nurse coordinator taught the child care teachers how to give Elliot his medications, monitor his health, and respond if he has a seizure. Sean and Jolie are now ready to make new friends and explore their new community.

Joseph and Elizabeth Carmina had it all worked out. Elizabeth was going to stay home with the children until their youngest, Charlie, was in kindergarten. Joseph made sure he had some time with each child individually: riding bikes or fishing with 5-year-old Craig on weekend afternoons, t-ball and ice cream with 4-year-old Maddie on Tuesdays, and swimming classes with Charlie on Saturday mornings. During these times, Elizabeth might do something special with the other children. On other occasions, she would take time for herself. The Carmina family has a lot of friends and extended family nearby, which means there's always a babysitter available. One day, Joseph was laid off from his job because of downsizing.

The stories above show how every family is unique, works in its own way, and has its own set of challenges. Each family is made up of different individuals, with their own characteristics and goals in life that can affect the entire family. For example, Jolie's career aspirations are important to her and play a part in the decisions the family makes, like moving to a new city. Each family as a whole also has goals to meet (for example, financial resources) and a vision of how they want their family to work. These visions may look different in different families. For example, the Carminas decided that Elizabeth would stay home with the children until school age. For the Simmons-Crause family, Jolie and Sean decided the boys would attend center-based child care. Family members work together to achieve the priorities of the entire family, as well as those of each individual family member. These priorities are identified and defined by each family. Early intervention supports families in meeting their priorities. Now, one might think, early intervention is about infants and toddlers with developmental delays and disabilities. Why would a program focused on child learning and development also think about the family's priorities? This is an important question.

WHY FOCUS ON THE FAMILY?

It might be easy to assume that early intervention focuses on the entire family "to be nice" or simply to "help out" families. But, in fact, early intervention supports the whole family because of two, interrelated reasons: 1.) the child is a member of the family, and 2.) the family has a significant impact on the child's development.

The first reason is simply that the child is a part of his or her family. It is within the family that the child lives, learns, and grows. Each family member influences one other. All family members are happy when one family member achieves a success, such as a promotion. And all family members are concerned when one family member has a disappointment, such as failing a test. The family as a whole is affected by what happens to one family member. With a pay raise, perhaps the family decides to buy a house where everyone will have their own room. Or with a failed test, perhaps the entire family finds a way to help that child study, such as taking over some of the child's chores or tutoring the child instead of watching television. For Sean and Jolie, if they did not find quality care for the boys, one of them might have stayed home to care for them. While this might have been possible financially, it would not have been ideal for this family, as both parents value their careers. Therefore, what happens to the family happens to the child. When the family works well, the child, as a member of the family, benefits.

Let's look more closely at the vital role families play in promoting child development. Family members are the ones who interact the most with their child. They create the opportunities for learning. They are responsible for keeping their child healthy and safe.[1] As discussed in Chapter 2, these components are vital to child learning. Routine activities are where learning opportunities occur, through the everyday interactions between the child and his or her family. These opportunities also occur during the routine activities children have without their families, such as in child care or at a neighbor's house during a play date. Even when learning experiences occur without other family members, it is the family who finds and schedules these opportunities so their child can explore, participate, and learn.[2]

The learning opportunities families provide are influenced by what else is going on in the family.[3] When the needs of family members are addressed, they can focus more readily on helping their child learn. For example, if Joseph and Elizabeth Carmina are spending all their time and energy thinking about what they will do for money and employment, they might not have the time or energy to help Charlie learn. If they are concerned about money, they might decide they can't afford t-ball and swimming classes. And they may also be too preoccupied to figure out how their children's interests could be met without these classes. While Sean and Jolie have friends and family from home who provide emotional support, they would like to make new friends in their community, preferably friends with young children. Together, the families could discuss their children's development, exchange advice on toys and daily care needs, and share places where their children could participate and learn. The opportunities to interact with other families would positively impact their parenting and their children's development.

A common assumption is that families only need support when they have significant concerns, such as the Carminas currently do. But just because families do not have major issues to deal with does not mean that there aren't priorities the family would like to address to better their family.[4] Think about New Year resolutions. Making New Year resolutions does not mean life isn't going well. Resolutions are simply goals to improve oneself or priorities for the coming year. Think of family priorities as New Year resolutions. The Simmons-Crause family had the emotional support needed during that first year, and financially they could afford for one of them to stay home. But they still have priorities around making new friends and succeeding in their careers. Therefore, families do not need to have misfortunes to have priorities they want to achieve. They have goals that, when addressed, allow family members to feel better about themselves and, in turn, the family functions better.

Research has shown that positive family functioning—families who feel good about how they're meeting their family goals—is related to positive child learning and development.[5] Specifically, child development is promoted when families have:

- people the family trusts and can rely on for help and advice (such as new friends who know the community and are also parenting and family and friends who frequently babysit);
- positive relationships among family members (such as parents who agree on how to raise their children);
- a sense of fulfillment and well-being of each family member (such as moving ahead in their careers and meeting the parenting goal of staying home with their children); and

- positive ways to parent their child (such as attending to a child's health care needs and spending quality one-on-one time with each child).[6]

The early intervention family–professional partnership identifies and finds ways to meet any priorities for which the family would like support. That way, families "have the time, energy, knowledge, and skills to provide their children with learning opportunities and experiences that promote child competence and development."[7]

FAMILIES OF CHILDREN
WITH DEVELOPMENTAL DELAYS OR DISABILITIES

All families have their ups and downs. Sometimes, families feel like they're running smoothly, like Sean and Jolie feel now that life is settled. And sometimes, families go through rough patches, such as the Carminas are encountering. In both stories, there was a time of change. While the boys' birth was a happy occasion, this change still required an adjustment as Sean and Jolie figured out how their family would work best. The Carminas are figuring out how their family might have to adjust to the change in Joseph's employment.

All families make adjustments to how their family works based on the changes that come about in their lives.[8] When a child enters the family—through birth, adoption, or marriage of blended families—there is a time of adjustment. The family learns the characteristics of this new family member (the child) and how the family will work with this new addition. For example, sleep schedules and time with friends are almost always altered with the birth of a baby. Families make changes as their children grow and have different needs, such as the plan for Elizabeth Carmina to go back to work after Charlie goes to kindergarten. Families make changes based on the child's strengths, interests, and needs. For example, a family might figure out that their baby really likes to stick to a schedule. So the family makes sure that their day is planned for the baby to eat and sleep when expected. To accommodate Maddie's t-ball schedule, Joseph Carmina used to go to work early on Tuesdays so he could take her. Families alter how their family works in ways that make sense for the child and for the family as a whole.

Early intervention supports families in meeting the priorities of their family, their child, and each family member. This does not mean that families of children with disabilities cannot handle what happens in their lives.[9] In fact, research has shown that families of children with developmental delays or disabilities make *positive* changes to how their family works and their routine activities based on their child's characteristics.[10] For example, Jolie and Sean took more parental leave than expected when the boys were born to focus on their health and developmental needs. The boys were already slotted in the infant class at the corporate child care center before they were born. But Sean and Jolie felt they needed to make sure that the center would still be a positive experience for the boys. This depended on how the teachers responded to Elliot's seizure diagnosis. These kinds of changes are the kinds that all families make for the good of their child. In this case, they just happen to be because of their children's unique health and developmental needs. Research has shown that families can and do make changes that consider both the needs of the child and their entire family.[11] That way, their family works the way they want it to, aligned with the important values, traditions, and expectations that make up their individual family culture.[12]

So, what would families do without early intervention? Based on the research described above, they would most likely do what all families do: figure out a way to get their priorities met. But families of children with developmental delays and disabilities do have additional considerations.[13] While all families support their child's learning and development, families of children with developmental delays or disabilities need to learn about the way their child communicates, interacts, and explores, which could be different from how other children do. Families of children with developmental delays or disabilities need to figure out learning and care strategies that might not be as obvious as those for typically developing children. Consider the extra tasks Sean and Jolie need to think about. They keep track of Elliot's medication schedule and document seizures. They coordinate with the child care teachers. They partner with a nurse coordinator and a neurologist as medical specialists. They partner with early intervention to find the best ways to interact with and promote Aiden and Elliot's development. This is in addition to the multiple tasks of all modern, busy families. With these extra priorities, families of children with developmental delays and disabilities could benefit from early intervention to: 1.) provide specialized resources related to their child's special needs, and 2.) brainstorm how to meet more general priorities typical of any family. Early intervention is available to support families as they work toward the best course for their entire family, considering the needs and priorities of all its members, including the child with developmental delays or disabilities.

FAMILY PRIORITIES AND RESOURCES

Joseph Carmina quickly lined up a new contract position after he lost his job, but questions remained. The family's health insurance from his previous employer would run out soon. Should Elizabeth take a position so the family would have health insurance? If so, who would care for Charlie and Maddie? Elizabeth is a nurse and might be able to find a position coordinating care from home, but she would have to make sure that benefits (such as health insurance) were available. Spending individual time with the children was important to Joseph.

Will he still be able to do all the activities with the children? He most likely could still do the weekend activities, but wondered about the weekdays, as he would be traveling frequently.

Aiden and Elliot easily transitioned into their child care classroom. In the morning, Jolie drops off the boys and gives the teachers a chart to document when Elliot receives his medication and any seizures that occur. She updates the teachers on any changes in Elliot's health since the previous day. In the afternoon, Sean picks up the boys and reviews the chart with the teachers. They bring the charts to the neurologist and their pediatrician at every appointment. Since the weekdays are very busy, the Simmons-Crause family explores their new city on the weekends. They have found a nearby park with equipment appropriate for infants. They go there once a week, hoping to meet other families with young children. They haven't made any connections yet, but are still hopeful.

All families have priorities. Priorities are the goals and visions the family hopes for. Priorities are also the everyday needs of the family. Common types of priorities are:

- feeling good about oneself and one's successes;
- emotional, social, and spiritual connections;
- money and everyday care needs;
- learning; and
- having free time to do what one enjoys, such as hobbies, sports, or relaxation.[14]

Most families routinely meet their priorities. But sometimes, those needs can suddenly be unmet, as the Carminas are currently experiencing. For most families, they are frequently thinking about new priorities or next steps, going to kindergarten, getting in shape, or making new friends. As seen in the above stories, family members coordinate with each other and use their family's *resources* to meet these priorities.

Resources can be a family member's internal strengths, such as Jolie's drive to get ahead in her career or Elizabeth's creativity in finding a job she can do from home. Resources are also supports available in the home and community. These resources can be informal or casual, and come from family, friends, and the community. Informal resources include the family and friends who babysit for the Caraminas, the flexibility available in Joseph's previous job to take off early on Tuesdays, the neighborhood park with infant equipment, and the learning opportunities of biking and fishing (for Craig Carmina). Resources can also be formal supports: agencies, programs or activities specifically designed to provide supports. Formal resources include the twin's center-based child care, Elliot's neurologist and nurse coordinator, and the learning opportunities of a t-ball league (for Maddie Carmina) and swimming class (for Charlie Carmina). Early intervention is also a formal resource. Families use the resources they have and know about to achieve their priorities. The resources families want to use will depend on the culture and values of the individual family. Table 3.1 lists some of the priorities of the families in the above stories, and how they go about meeting them. Some of the priorities are already occurring. The priorities marked with a dagger (†) are those the families are currently figuring out. Early intervention can support families in meeting their priorities by providing resources that make sense within the individual family's culture.

Table 3.1. Family Priorities for the Simmons-Crause and Carmina Families

Priorities	Simmons-Crause Family	Carmina Family
Feeling Good About Oneself	• Jolie's new position prompting their move	• Elizabeth staying home as envisioned
Emotional/ Social Supports	• Long-distance friends and family • Making friends in a new city †	• Friends and family nearby
Learning Opportunities	• Home • Child care • Neighborhood park	• Home • Maddie's t-ball • Charlie's swimming class • Craig fishing and biking
Financial Resources	• Two-family income	• Joseph's income • Joseph begins a contract position † • Elizabeth is looking into home-based work options †
Child Care	• Center-based child care	• Family and friends • Need more so Elizabeth can work †
Time as a Family	• Weekends	• Joseph has individual time with each child • Able to attend Maddie's t-ball games †
Free Time	• Exploring the new city †	• Elizabeth getting some alone time
Health Care	• Neurologist and pediatrician • Family's nurse-coordinator prepared child care teachers to administer Elliot's medications and respond to a seizure • Internist for adults • Coordinate with teachers to track seizures and update medication changes and questions about seizure procedures †	• Pediatrician • Family Practitioner for adults

† The family is currently working on ways to meet these priorities.

What does the word *needs* mean? Some might think of needs as a weakness, something negative that only families in crisis have. But actually, all individuals have needs. A baby needs opportunities to play and explore. A teenager who wants to drive needs a driver's license. A college student needs money for tuition and books. Adults need time to relax and be able to achieve what's important to them. Needs are not the same as weaknesses or deficits. Needs are anything that help people feel satisfied, good about themselves, and successful. A family's hopes, dreams, visions, and needs are all important priorities. These priorities are individualized to the family and are only priorities if the family considers them so. What priorities does early intervention support? Whichever priorities the family wants to address through early intervention so that they can be available and ready to help their child learn and develop.[15]

FAMILY-DRIVEN EARLY INTERVENTION OUTCOMES

In any family's life, there are many priorities they feel quite comfortable managing themselves. But there can be other priorities that early intervention might support. The family–professional partnership identifies those priorities. From there, family outcomes are made, which are expected to be achieved by participating in early intervention.

There are two kinds of family outcomes. Family outcomes might be related to the child, such as finding quality child care so a parent can return to work. This is a parenting outcome. Or, family outcomes might be less directly related to the child, such as the parent who is returning to work deciding on the kind of job she might find fulfilling. This is a family outcome. *Parenting outcomes* are priorities that families address as the parent of a child, or specifically the parent of a child with developmental delays or disabilities. Parenting outcomes include creating learning opportunities, coordinating health and child care, and helping others understand the child's special needs. *Family outcomes* are those priorities that are for the family in general, and other family members. Family outcomes include finding some alone time, meeting career aspirations, and relying on friends for emotional and social support.

The description of potential family and parenting outcomes may seem a little vague. Since each family is so individual, their priorities and the effect on child development is hard to define.[16] However, the U.S. federal government funded the Early Childhood Outcomes (ECO) Center to explore the outcomes that should be expected from participating in early intervention. Like the child outcomes described in Chapter 2, the ECO Center identified five family outcomes.[17] Table 3.2 lists these outcomes, and provides a description and example for each outcome. While these are expected outcomes in general, the priorities that families have, and want to share with early intervention, are unique for every family, and change based on the current priorities of the family.

Table 3.2. Early Childhood Outcomes (ECO) Center Family Outcomes Expected from Early Intervention

Outcome	Definition	Examples
Families understand child's strengths, abilities, and special needs	• Knows child's unique learning characteristics, temperament, interests, etc. • Identifies special considerations for child's health and development†	• Sean and Jolie would like to know more about long-term implications of Elliot's seizures on his learning and development
Families know their rights and advocate effectively for their children	• Understands and obtains supports expected from early intervention and other health, developmental, and social programs • Speaks on behalf of their children and other children with developmental delays and disabilities	• Joseph and Elizabeth want to be able to talk about Charlie's development to others so that Charlie is accepted in his classes and the community in general
Families help their child develop and learn	• Interacts with and engages child in learning opportunities • Provides materials and settings that are safe and promote learning • Partners with early intervention and other professionals to ensure appropriate developmental recommendations	• Joseph wants to find another time to spend with Maddie because he can't go to t-ball games • Sean and Jolie want to find learning opportunities in their new city
Families have support systems	• Has informal and formal resources they can use to help meet their family and parenting priorities	• Elizabeth wants to figure out how she can find more hours of babysitting even if she works from home
Families access desired services, programs, and activities in their community	• Knows and uses community resources that suit their family, including child care and other developmental programs, health and social supports, and community-based activities	• Sean and Jolie continue to coordinate with teachers on seizures and medication changes • Sean and Jolie want to join a "parents of multiples" group

† Bailey, Bruder, Hebbler, Carta, Defosset, et al., 2006

IDENTIFYING FAMILY AND PARENTING OUTCOMES

Family and parenting outcomes result from a conversation between the family and early intervention professional. There are a variety of tools that can be used to guide the conversation. Some tools are surveys with specific examples of potential areas for support. While these tools may be helpful in identifying areas that the family–professional partnership might discuss, they might not be the best way for most families to identify their priorities. A more open-ended conversation can uncover the family's individual priorities and particular outcomes.[18] This conversation could be free-flowing, or a semistructured guide could be used. With or without a guide, the family–professional partnership can discuss:

Who is a part of the family? What are the family's values? How does this particular family work? This provides the family–professional partnership with a clear understanding of the individual family. The family identifies its members, what's important to them, and the ways they prefer to meet their goals. For example, the Carminas prefer to use informal resources to meet their child care needs.

What are the priorities for the entire family? What are the priorities for each member of the family? This identifies the different aspects of family life the family is thinking about. These aspects begin to identify specific outcomes for the family–professional partnership to achieve. For example, the Carminas' priority is to find employment for Elizabeth that provides health insurance.

What does the priority look like for this family? How will the family know when each priority is achieved? This considers the family's individual values and preferences for meeting the priority. For the Carminas, the outcome and ways to meet the outcome are tailored to the family's preference that the children stay home and are cared for by a parent until kindergarten.

How is the family currently trying to fulfill those priorities? What resources does the family already have? This identifies the family's plan or ideas for meeting their priorities, and resources available to address them. For example, Elizabeth is hoping to work in the evenings when Joseph is home, and during the day when the children are napping. But there will be times when she will need to work when the children need her time and attention. The Carminas have the resource of many friends and family members who can watch the children when needed. That way, Elizabeth can focus on work and not worry about the children. The Carminas are calling them to know their availability before Elizabeth interviews for particular positions. Elizabeth also knows of another resource—a nurse recruiter—who could help her find a home-based position.

What else does the family need to achieve these priorities? Are there certain areas that early intervention can help with to achieve these priorities? In light of the family's plan and resources, this considers what else is needed. The family–professional partnership identifies how early intervention can support the family's priority. For example, the Carminas think that there might be certain days or times that their family and friends won't be able to cover. There might be some unexpected times they will need child care. They also don't want to ask too much of their friends and family. Keeping with the family's needs, and their interest in informal sources of support, the early intervention professional suggests a college student majoring in child development. A college student's hours could be flexible and, except for class times, could be available with little notice.

Through this conversation, the family–professional partnership identifies the family's priorities and ways to meet them based on the family's values and culture. Could the Carminas have met this outcome without the support of early intervention? Most likely, they could. But the early intervention professional thought of a possible resource the Carminas might not have. The family–professional partnership pools its resources to best meet the priorities of the family.

THE FAMILY–PROFESSIONAL PARTNERSHIP:
OUTCOMES AND APPROACHES

Regardless of the specific priority, the family–professional partnership finds ways to achieve the expected outcome. If needed, the partnership connects families with resources the family does not currently have or been able to get.[19] The family–professional partnership best meets these priorities when they think about *what* is provided, the early intervention resources; and *how* supports are provided, the way the family–professional partnership works together.[20]

Family–Professional Partnership Resources

The early intervention family–professional partnership joins forces to find and obtain resources that best fit the family's individual culture.[21] Families bring to the partnership their strengths and resources they already have (for example, the Carminas' family and friends) or know about (for example, nurse recruiter). Professionals bring to the partnership their own strengths and resources, as well as the resources they know about in the community and how to obtain them. The early intervention professional also has connections with other community resources to determine if a certain resource exists and where to find it. Therefore, early intervention does not have to know everything, nor provide all the resources. Instead, the professional is a *resource broker*, someone who knows what's available in the community and how to hook up families with those resources.[22]

The resources early intervention provides, or connects families to, might be specifically for families of children with developmental delays or disabilities. Or, the resources might be for any family regardless of the child's developmental status. Resources early intervention can provide that are specifically for families of children with developmental delays or disabilities include:

- information about the child's specific disability or development;
- adjustments to the family's routine;
- skills and material resources, such as specific equipment and supports in using it; and
- skills and other resources that aid families in feeling confident about parenting a child with special needs.[23]

For example, Sean and Jolie wanted to make sure that the child care center they chose could meet Elliot's unique needs. Their nurse coordinator supported them in making this decision. And, as discussed in Chapter 1, the Carminas wanted skills and knowledge in explaining Charlie's special needs to others. Patrice, their early intervention professional, worked with them to be able to do this.

Regardless of whether the family's priority is related to the child's diagnosis, resources early intervention can provide are:

- knowledge and skills;
- places to get reliable information;
- community supports;
- materials; and
- emotional supports.[24]

Table 3.3 provides two examples of each of these resources, one related to parenting outcomes and one related to family outcomes. With these resources, early intervention is providing families with informational, material, and emotional resources to help operate their family and parent their children.

When identifying resources, family–professional partnerships sometimes tend to go straight to formal resources, such as, agencies, programs, or classes.[25] However, informal resources are extremely valuable to families.[26] The family–professional partnership builds off the family's already existing informal resources. They also consider other informal resources—those everyday supports available to a family in the community—to meet their outcomes.[27] The family–professional partnership can be creative and think beyond "program." This provides a wider array of potential resources.

Table 3.3. Early Intervention Resources and Examples of Parenting and Family Outcomes

Resources	Parenting Outcome	Family Outcome
Knowledge and Skills	How to navigate child's health care	Ways to eat nutritiously
Information Sources	Reliable Web sites regarding child's disability †	Where to obtain a community directory of resources
Community Supports	Local child's gym Neighborhood play groups	Wellness seminars at the YMCA Neighborhood get-togethers
Material/Financial	Special equipment	Linking to a job recruiter
Emotional Supports	Meeting families of multiples	Joining a special interest club

† Turnbull, Turnbull, Erwin, & Soodak, 2006

Ways of Partnering

Notice the words used to describe how the family–professional partnership works: *supports, connects, assists*. Early intervention is not about "doing for" families, but giving families what they need to do for themselves. Early intervention is not about telling families what to do, but providing information and other resources so the family can make informed decisions for their own family. By partnering with the family, the professional learns about resources the professional might not have thought of before, and learns more about how individual families work. The professional becomes better equipped to meet the priorities of this family and future families. The family becomes armed with new strengths and community resources to meet their current priority, and have the knowledge, skills, and other resources to meet future priorities.

Research has found that *how* early intervention is provided is as important as *what* is provided.[28] Early intervention leadership recommends a true partnership between family and professionals. A family–professional partnership is defined as:

> A relationship in which families (not just parents) and professionals agree to defer to each other's judgments and expertise, as appropriate for the purpose of securing benefits for [children], other family members, and professionals.[29]

The family–professional partnership collaborates in the planning and implementation of early intervention.[30] That is, the partners pool their knowledge and expertise to come to the best decisions for the particular family. Since the family is ultimately affected by the decisions made, the family chooses the resources that best fit their priorities and the way their family works.[31] The professional helps the family make that choice by sharing information and brainstorming the pros and cons of using different resources.

Research has also found that early intervention is more helpful to families when the family–professional partnership works in the way an informal resource is usually provided.[32] The early intervention professional interacts with the family in a casual and friendly manner, and is viewed as an ally who might have the inside scoop on specific information and other resources. Early intervention does not view families as having concerns that require fixing. Instead, early intervention professionals partner with families to find the best way to meet the priorities they envision for their family, their child, and other family members.

Family Outcomes Option

Even though early intervention provides the option of focusing on family and parenting outcomes, families may choose to focus only on developmental outcomes for their child. There are a few possible reasons for this. First, families may feel they don't need early intervention supports to meet their family's priorities. Or, given the child's developmental needs, families may be focused on these needs and might not have considered other family priorities.[33] The family–professional partnership can leave the door open to address family priorities as they arise, and revisit the option from time to time.[34] That way, family outcomes can be addressed if, or when, the time is right. In other situations, families may feel uncomfortable addressing family priorities. They may feel like they're being judged.[35] The family–professional partnership can have open and honest conversations about why family outcomes are sometimes addressed in early intervention. That said, families do not have to share their family's priorities and can choose not to address any family priorities through early intervention.

THE BIG PICTURE:
RELATED POLICIES AND GUIDELINES

The concepts described in this chapter are also reflected in early intervention policies and recommended practices. These guidelines help the family–professional partnership create early intervention plans that meet the individual priorities of the entire family and each of its members. That way, the family can attend to parenting in general, and helping their child learn specifically.

Addressing family priorities are intentionally outlined in the early intervention legislation of Part C of the Individuals with Disabilities Education Act (IDEA). The legislation states that the family–professional partnership identifies "the resources, priorities, and concerns of the family and the identification of the supports and services necessary to enhance the family's capacity to meet the developmental needs of the infant or toddler."[36] The regulations further specify that a family-directed, open-ended "interview" (that is, conversation) is used to identify family priorities.[37] Additionally, state early intervention programs are required to report on how early intervention has helped families in three of the ECO Center's family outcomes. States need to identify whether "early intervention services have helped the family: 1.) know their rights; 2.) effectively communicate their children's needs; and 3.) help their children develop and learn."[38] In order for states to report this, each family–professional partnership uses specific tools and procedures (chosen by the state) to document whether early intervention has helped families with these outcomes.

Recognizing the critical role families play in child learning and development, the Division for Early Childhood of the Council for Exceptional Children (DEC) recommends family-based early intervention practices.[39] These practices include both the outcomes and approaches described in the previous sections, and the importance of the family–professional partnership in meeting child developmental outcomes. The recommended practices emphasize:

- family–professional collaboration in identifying and achieving outcomes;
- supports that build on family strengths and align with the family's individual culture, preferences, and way of life; and
- a focus on informal and formal resources that are "supportive and do not disrupt family and community life."[40]

When early intervention occurs according to policies and recommended practices, the family–professional partnership is best suited to effectively support family priorities.

SUMMARY: FOR THE FAMILY, FOR THE CHILD

All families have hopes, visions, and needs. All families, including those with children with identified developmental delays or disabilities, have strengths and other resources to meet these priorities. The early intervention family–professional partnership jointly identifies family priorities and resources, and any additional resources the family could use, to meet those priorities. When these priorities are addressed, the family is available and able to help the child learn and develop in everyday life.

Chapter 4

THE CHILD, IMPORTANT PEOPLE, AND PARTICULAR PLACES

The Liangs were more than ready to bring their daughter, Jia, home from the hospital. After she was born, Jia spent 4 weeks in the Neonatal Intensive Care Unit (NICU) to address a medical issue with her heart. The Liang family was automatically eligible for early intervention because Jia had a diagnosis of Down syndrome. Before leaving the hospital, the Liang family, hospital NICU staff, and local early intervention professionals met to create the intervention plan. That way, early intervention at home could begin immediately. The intervention outcomes focused on Jia eating, coping with sights and sounds, and interacting with her family. At the first home visit, the Liang family and Danicka, an occupational therapist, discussed how things were going overall, and specifically how Jia was participating in routine activities at home. When Danicka arrived at the Liang's house, Jia was sleeping. The Liangs explained that Jia sleeps a lot and it would be hard to really know when she might wake up. Danicka assured the Liangs that they could use this time to talk about Jia's learning and development. They could discuss what Jia was doing in routine activities, and what her parents were doing to help her participate and learn. If Jia woke up, Danicka would watch some of the routine activities. The conversation started with the beginning of the day. For each routine activity, the family talked about what the activity looked like, what Jia does during that time, and how else she might participate.

The Cabrera family, introduced in Chapter 2, has been participating in early intervention for about 10 months. Eighteen-month-old Franco spends 3 days a week at child care and 2 days a week at home with his father. One of the routine activities focused on during intervention visits is eating at home and at child care. Specifically, Franco is learning to eat with a spoon, ask for more, and learn responsibility by clearing his place. Kevin, a speech pathologist, visits Franco's home and child care during different meals—breakfast, lunch, and snack times—to support the family and Franco's teachers as they help Franco learn these competencies. At the beginning of each intervention visit, whether at home or in child care, Kevin and the adults responsible for Franco's learning and development discuss how things have been going since Kevin's last visit. They talk about how Franco's learning the identified competencies and the strategies the adults have used to help him learn. After the team catches up, Kevin watches the routine activity to see how it's going.

As discussed in Chapter 2, infants and toddlers learn and develop in the routine activities in which they participate during their everyday life. Through these routine activities, they use the competencies they've mastered, practice the ones they're working on, and have an opportunity to try those they are not yet doing. But specifically, what should each child learn in those routine activities? How does the early intervention team know what to work on? What should the focus be? What types of help should early intervention provide?

Since each family and child is unique, there isn't a specific curriculum or existing plan that works for all families, or for those with similar characteristics. For example, just because a child has a diagnosis of autism does not mean that he or she needs the same intervention as all other children with autism. The early intervention supports for the Liangs will be different from any other family with a newborn who is diagnosed with Down syndrome and has medical concerns with her heart. This is also true for families with similar early intervention interests. For example, just because two families want strategies to help with challenging behaviors or to focus on learning opportunities while taking a bath, does not mean that the same plan or generic strategies will work for both children and both families. What early intervention will look like for the Cabrera family will be different from any other family, even if other families are looking for ways to promote eating, communicating wants, and learning responsibility during meal and snack times. There is no cookbook for early intervention. Each recipe is designed by the family–professional partnership.

Unlike creating a recipe, however, the early intervention partnership does not start from scratch. Things are already brewing. Children are already learning and participating in routine activities. Family members and other important people in the child's life are already interacting with their children. To figure out how early intervention can best support the family, the early intervention partnership first needs to know what's already happening. How is the child currently learning and participating in routine activities? What does the child already know how to do? How do the people, materials, and setting of routine activities affect what the child is learning and how the child is participating? The answers to these questions, which are discovered through *assessment*, create a picture of the child's current developmental strengths and needs, and the important people and particular places where a child learns.

EARLY INTERVENTION ASSESSMENT: AN OVERVIEW

Adults assess children all the time. Parents watch their child rocking back and forth on her hands and knees and discuss how soon she'll begin crawling. While on line at a store checkout, a baby in a shopping cart smiles and babbles at the customer behind him. The customer jokingly says, "He's very shy, isn't he," and the mother responds, "He's my flirt!" While stuck in traffic, a toddler riding in a car begins to cry. His father realizes that the toddler, who has limited vision, is probably bored and wondering what is going on. His father begins talking to him about all the cars with nowhere to go. These adults assessed the children's emerging competencies (crawling), personality and interaction style (flirtatious), and ways to engage the child by knowing his learning characteristics (describe what the child cannot see). In early intervention, assessments are done to meet the same purpose: to understand the child's development so that the important people in a child's life can help him or her learn.

The term *assessment* usually brings to mind a testing situation in a clinic or an office at one isolated moment in time. In fact, assessment continually happens in early intervention. It happens anytime the early intervention partnership wants to understand:

- what the child knows how to do;
- how well the child knows how to do it;
- how the child learns; and
- how well intervention strategies are working.

Assessment is used to understand child strengths, needs, interests, and competencies. Assessment is also about understanding how the people, objects, and settings that make up the child's routine activities "help a child make fullest use of his or her developmental potential."[1] Assessment begins by identifying the child's competencies in everyday life, and ends with interpreting what those competencies mean so that interventions can be planned.

Assessment Methods

How does the early intervention partnership gather this developmental information? There are many ways, but it occurs primarily by observing the child. Early intervention professionals might watch routine activities as they unfold. Kevin, for example, will watch Franco as he eats at home and child care. Early intervention professionals discuss their observations with the family and other team members. This can happen during the routine activity while the family is participating in the routine activity, or they can report back what they see if the family is not there. For example, Kevin might talk to the Cabreras while he's watching what's happening during breakfast. He might also talk to Franco's child care teachers while he's watching what's happening there. Kevin might also report back to the Cabreras what he saw at child care. The early intervention professionals are not the only ones observing. Family members also watch how their child participates in routine activities and share with other team members what they see happening.[2] Family members might observe routine activities they are a part of, or ones in which they usually do not participate. For example, Danicka asked the Liangs to describe what happens throughout their daily routine activities. But they might also discuss how Jia responded when blood was drawn in the NICU, an activity her parents watched, but did not participate in. Research has found that family members can and do provide accurate and important information about their child's learning and development.[3] Early intervention professionals have the tools to support families by asking the "right" questions. That way, families can describe their child's participation so that everyone understands the child's learning and development.

Sometimes, the early intervention partnership might use specific instruments to help guide the assessment process. Assessment instruments outline the different skills that comprise a developmental domain or competency, and are usually ordered from early skills to more sophisticated ones. Some instruments compare what a child can do to what other children can do at the same age. Others compare a child's competencies to an age range in which those competencies usually develop. And some instruments do not make any comparisons, but instead provide an outline of potential competencies that guide the observations and identify new competencies to learn. Each instrument has specific guidelines on how to use them, which might include the early intervention professional observing the child, discussing with families and other important caregivers what they see, or asking the child to do specific tasks. While these instruments can help the family–professional partnership assess a child's learning and development, they are only one piece of the many sources of information that come together to create a clear, complete picture of a child's learning and development. As the Division for Early Childhood, Council for Exceptional Children (DEC) recommended practices state, "tests do not make decisions—people do."[4]

Reasons for Assessments

There are many reasons to assess a child's development in early intervention. Assessments are used to determine if a family is eligible for early intervention.[5] As discussed in Chapter 1, there are many ways families can be eligible. If a child has an "established condition" or certain "risk factor(s)" defined by the state early intervention program, the question of eligibility is easily answered. Since Jia has a diagnosis of Down syndrome, the family is considered presumptively, or automatically, eligible for early intervention.[6] For other families, however, additional assessment is needed to decide whether a child's current developmental profile can be defined as delayed. Remember Charlie Carmina from Chapter 1? His family was concerned that Charlie was not developing the same way his older siblings did at his age. The early intervention team needed to determine if Charlie's current development was delayed based on the early intervention program's definition of delay. So, Jessica and Patrice from the local early intervention agency and Charlie's parents did an *eligibility evaluation*. Jessica and Patrice asked questions about Charlie's health and what he does when he plays and participates in family routine activities. They watched Charlie in some of those routine activities, discussed his parent's thoughts on Charlie's development, and documented the information on different assessment instruments so that the family–professional partnership could determine eligibility.

Another reason for assessment is to understand the child's learning characteristics so interventions can be planned.[7] The family–professional partnership is trying to decide, "Given the child's learning characteristics, what is the best way to help the child meet developmental outcomes?" and "What can early intervention provide to the family as they help their child learn?" This type of assessment was used with both the Liangs and the Carminas. During that first home visit, Danicka and the Liangs discussed how Jia participates in the routine activities of eating, coping, and interacting with her parents at home. Before the first intervention plan was developed, Jessica and Patrice observed the Carminas in the evening and the morning routines to see how Charlie learns and participates at those times, focusing on the family's priorities of play, mobility, and communication. By gathering this information, the early intervention partnership understands how Jia and Charlie learn and participate in their routine activities. From that, the partnership can identify steps and strategies to meet developmental goals.

The final reason assessments are typically used in early intervention is to determine how well the intervention is working.[8] The early intervention partnership wants to understand, "Is the child learning the competencies the family wants the child to learn?" and "Is the family happy with the strategies used?" These questions are continually asked and answered during intervention visits. In between intervention visits, the family is continually evaluating (or assessing) how well the strategies are helping their child learn and how they feel about using those strategies. This is what Kevin and the adults in Franco's life are doing during the intervention visits. As Franco grows and develops, the early intervention partnership of the Cabrera family, Kevin, and Franco's child care teachers will determine whether the strategies need to change because Franco's new competencies require new strategies, or the strategies can stay the same because they can still help Franco as he learns new competencies. If Franco does not progress, then the early intervention partnership needs to determine why he isn't progressing and change the approach based on this assessment information.

The process of conducting assessments will look different for each of the three reasons discussed above. For example, in eligibility determination, the assessment may focus more on global developmental expectations to determine if a delay exists, while assessment to develop an intervention plan will be more focused on the specific competencies and learning style of the child in routine activities. And assessment for determining the effectiveness of interventions will be specific to the intervention goals or outcomes. For all of these reasons, the common purpose of assessment is to learn more about how the child learns and participates in his or her everyday life. Family members and early intervention professionals who participate in assessments learn more about what the child's behaviors mean, the child's strengths and needs, and how best to support the child's learning and development.[9] The information gathered is meaningful to the family so they can support their child's development as they envisioned for their family.

FAMILY VISION AND GOALS

As described in Chapter 2, children learn both the developmental competencies expected of infants and toddlers, and the family's values and culture. What each child learns depends on what is important to that child's family. Therefore, the family–professional partnership needs to identify what those priorities are so the assessment is aligned with them. What does the family hope to achieve through early intervention? What are their goals for their child? Are there certain developmental competencies concerning the family? Are there certain competencies they value and would like to promote? Each family identifies the specific developmental competencies, values, and cultural expectations they want their child to learn, and early intervention to support. Examples of the priorities are:

- Developmental competencies: Play or engage with toys
- Values: Learn to take care of the environment by helping with recycling
- Cultural expectations: Take off one's shoes before entering the house

These priorities are important to know so that, during the assessment, the child's current development and learning style can be explored in relation to this vision.

Let's look at the different types of goals the Liangs came up with for Jia. They wanted to focus on eating because Jia was having a difficult time. She was spilling a lot of formula and became exhausted because it was so hard. The Liangs also wanted to focus on coping with sights and sounds, known as *regulation*. Jia handled the busyness of the NICU quite well and the Liangs thought that this skill could help her deal with changes to routines and new situations. Therefore, they wanted to keep promoting this competency. Finally, the Liangs wanted to focus on interaction. They envisioned a child who they could smile back and forth with, talk softly to who would respond by smiling and snuggling, and touch as they "spoke" through these interactions. Each of the Liang's priorities arose for different reasons. They show that a priority might come about due to:

- A developmental concern (for example, Jia eating).
- A developmental strength (for example, Jia's regulatory competence).
- An important vision (for example, quiet face-to-face interactions between Jia and her parents).

Families can identify any goals they want to focus on in early intervention. Goals can be a concern, but they can also be developmental strengths or a vision the family has for their child and their family.

Some families in early intervention might say their vision for their child is "to develop like she or he is supposed to" or "be like other kids his or her age." These certainly could be the family's vision. Some children in early intervention will meet this vision, while other children might not. Infant and toddler development is very unpredictable, making it difficult to ultimately know a child's developmental course. The family's vision can change over time as the child's development unfolds. Some families might identify priorities related to general developmental milestones, such as to walk, eat, talk, learn, or be social. These are certainly goals that most families would want for their children. However, to focus the assessment on specific priorities for the individual child and family, these generic goals are translated into the family's life and the child's characteristics. Specific priorities for each family and child can be shaped by identifying what goals might look like in the more immediate future—what the child might learn—and in the routine activities of the family. These more specific outcomes expected to be achieved by early intervention are determined by discussing "What would that look like?" or "What could she learn to do now?" or "How do you see her participating?" The conversation among the family–professional partnership results in outcomes unique and tailored to the characteristics of each family and child.

In order to identify the family's priorities that guide the assessment, the family brings to the family–professional partnership their vision for their child—what they want their child to learn—which only they know. Early intervention professionals bring to the partnership ways to support the family in identifying that vision, and describing competencies the child could learn as he or she develops toward the family's vision. There are a variety of ways to identify family priorities for their child, and different tools that can help. For example, Connecticut's early intervention program has a Hopes and Dreams Exercise that families can complete to prepare for this conversation (http://www.birth23.org/Families/hopeseng.pdf/). Robin McWilliam, an early intervention researcher, designed the Routines Based Interview that can be used as a guide for identifying family goals for their child by looking at what happens during their typical routine activities. [10] With or without the use of a tool, the early intervention partnership identifies the family's vision for their child. Let's use the Liang family from the beginning of this chapter and the Carmina family from Chapter 1 to explore how this conversation might happen.

Since the Liangs identified their priorities and goals while still in the NICU, they could only envision what their routine activities would look like when they took Jia home. So, the early intervention partnership decided to identify developmental competencies the family thought were important for Jia to learn. The conversation centered on the following questions:

- What does the family want Jia to learn or be able to do?
- What has Jia already learned to do or she is really good at learning how to do?
- What are family traditions, or everyday customs or practices, the family does? Are these important for Jia to learn?
- What are family values—their principles or morals—they want to teach Jia?

The priorities of eating, coping, and interacting resulted from this conversation. These competencies were further defined because they will be different for each family and child. For example, the Liangs described interaction as back and forth communication, looking into each other's eyes, vocalizing, and touching. Another family might think of interaction as playing together with rattles and other toys. The early intervention partnership clarifies the priorities based on the family's vision of what this competency would look like.

For the Carmina family, Charlie has been participating in everyday routine activities since he was born. Therefore, the early intervention partnership decided to start with routine activities to identify specific developmental goals. The first part of the conversation centered on the following questions:

- What do the Carminas see as important times of the day when Charlie can learn?
- What are routine activities Charlie likes? What are routine activities Charlie dislikes?
- What are routine activities the family would like to do, or would like Charlie to do, but has not figured out how Charlie can participate?
- What does Charlie's day look like? What does he do first? And then? [11]

From these kinds of questions, the conversation moves to what Charlie can learn or is learning within those routine activities.

Some families might expect the early intervention professionals—as the *professionals*—to identify developmental areas of concern that need to be addressed.

While early intervention professionals can collaborate with families to identify each child's unique strengths and needs, the priorities or goals go beyond the general developmental knowledge the early intervention professional brings. The professional can help understand the child's development, but only the family can identify what's most important to their family. Together, the family–professional partnership creates a picture of the child's development by conducting an assessment tailored to the unique family culture in which the child lives, learns, and grows.

THE TROUBLE WITH TRADITIONAL TESTS AND RECOMMENDED APPROACHES

Let's look at part of a traditional early childhood assessment. A baby, on her parent's lap or by herself, sits at a table or on the floor opposite an early intervention professional. The professional asks the baby to "point to" specific pictures in a book. The baby has never seen the book before, so the baby picks it up to explore. The professional gives the baby some time to look at the book, and then asks her again to point to pictures. The parent tells the professional that the baby can point to pictures in books at home. The professional says she is happy to hear that, but the baby is expected to point to pictures in this particular book in order to score that skill on the assessment instrument. The professional then shows the baby a small toy. The baby reaches out for it and the professional hides it under a cup. The baby looks at her parent, who tells her to get the toy. The baby lifts the cup and begins to "drink" out of the cup. The professional documents that the baby did not pass either item on the test.

For a long time, young children's development was assessed this way. Developmental specialists across disciplines would give children objects and tell them to do something with the object. Tasks included putting a string of beads in a tube, putting a toy in a variety of positions as directed by the professional (for example, on, in, between, in front of), and repeating sequences of numbers. In other words, the child was expected to perform "strange behavior[s] in strange situations with strange adults for the briefest possible period of time."[12]

Many aspects of traditional assessments are simply not appropriate for young children. Infants and toddlers are expected to comply with directions instead of explore and interact with objects and others in their own way.[13] Items are scored as not passed when the child might simply have no interest in the expected task. Young children are expected to stay in one place for a much longer period of time than is recommended.[14] Also, traditional assessments usually do not allow for different ways to express the same skill, such as if a child looks at a named picture but does not point to, or touch the picture.

A major limitation of traditional assessments is that the competencies a child demonstrates, or does not demonstrate, are not necessarily the competencies a child can or cannot do in everyday life. For young children, this is especially true because of the issue with generalization discussed in Chapter 2. In fact, traditional assessments are trying to bring out the developmental competencies infants and toddlers learn and use in everyday life. For the infant in the example above, the assessor was trying to see if the child knows the names of different objects in pictures and understands the concept of object permanence, knowing that something exists even if she does not see it. But, instead of trying to make the child show these competencies in unnatural situations, why not see what the child can do in her routine activities? After all, it is within everyday life that families see areas of concern that prompt them to seek early intervention in the first place. So why not let the child point to pictures in her own book at her own house with her mother, as it usually occurs? Why not see if the child shows an understanding of object permanence in everyday life by perhaps:

- Looking for a ball in a toy box. (She is showing that she knows the ball is where she left it, even though she doesn't see it.)
- Looking under the table for the cup she dropped.
- Searching in the diaper bag for her pacifier.
- Going to her room to get her shoes when asked.
- Pointing to the refrigerator for juice.

Assessing children as they participate in the routine activities of real life is called *authentic* assessment.[15] Authentic assessment methods are different from traditional assessments in that development is understood according to how the child functions in everyday life, where it matters. No one has to assume erroneously that the competencies seen in traditional assessments generalize to the child's real life competencies. This method has been endorsed by early childhood professional associations.[16] In the next section, we will explore what is assessed to understand child learning and development within the context of everyday life.

CONSTRUCTING AN AUTHENTIC DEVELOPMENTAL PICTURE: CHILD, ENVIRONMENT, AND STRATEGIES

During that first home visit, the Liangs and Danicka discussed times when the family is interacting with Jia. Mrs. Liang described how she cradles Jia in her arms, strokes her hair, puts her finger in Jia's palm to grasp onto, and brings her face close to Jia's so they can look into each other's eyes. Danicka asked how Jia responds to these interactions. Mrs. Liang said that Jia loves to hold onto her finger and leans her head into her mother's hand when she strokes her hair. Jia will slowly look toward her mother, especially when her mother speaks softly to

Jia, but then turns away after a short period of time. Danicka asked what Mrs. Liang does when Jia turns away. Mrs. Liang responded that she waits for Jia to turn back, and will talk softly to her. Mrs. Liang said that she thinks Jia sometimes needs a break. Danicka agreed and explained that sometimes, even when babies are enjoying themselves, the stimulation can be too much and they become overwhelmed. It may be that Jia is using her strength in regulating so that when she feels overwhelmed, she turns away until she is ready to interact again. Danicka said that since Mrs. Liang is letting Jia take this time, Jia is continuing to learn to cope with stimulation and that she can join the interaction again when she is ready.

At the next intervention visit, Kevin came during lunch time, when it is just Roberto and Franco Cabrera at home. Kevin asked Roberto how this routine activity was going. Roberto said that Franco was doing so well eating from a spoon with thicker foods, like apple sauce, that Roberto began giving Franco thinner foods for lunch, most particularly soup. Roberto did, however, want Kevin to see if Roberto was "doing it right." Kevin said that there is no one right way, but he could certainly watch and discuss what he sees. Franco sat in his highchair, face to face with his father. Franco was very focused on eating. While Franco tried, his father held the bowl so Franco didn't spill. Once Franco scooped with the spoon, his father held Franco's hand until the spoon was near Franco's chin. Then, Roberto let go of the spoon and let Franco put the spoon in his mouth on his own. Franco looked at his father and smiled at his accomplishment.

A couple of days later, Kevin went to Franco's child care to see how snack was going. The children were eating small crackers with their fingers. Franco sat at the small table with his classmates on a toddler-sized chair. He frequently tried to gain his balance as he leaned off to one side of the chair. Kevin collaborated with Franco's teacher to see if a different chair might help his stability. The teacher found a chair with arm and foot rests. Franco enjoyed watching and interacting with his classmates as they ate. He picked up one of the crackers and brought it to his mouth. As he watched the other children, he missed his mouth and hit his cheek. He let go of the cracker, which fell to the floor.

In each of these stories, an assessment is being conducted. The assessments are focusing on the child's learning and development, how people, objects, and settings support the child's learning, and what strategies are used or could be used to further enhance learning and development.

Child Competencies

Child learning and development is the primary focus of assessment and is looked at in a functional way, how the child participates or engages in routine activities.[17] The focus is on what the child does and does not do in everyday life. So what is specifically assessed? It's the different developmental tasks of infancy and toddlerhood described in Chapter 2. The following questions can guide the assessment around those developmental tasks:

- What are the child's unique *strengths* and *interests*?
- How is the child *participating* or *engaging* in the activity? Could the child be *participating* more? How else could the child be *participating*? What competencies could the child learn so that he or she could *participate* more?
- What is the child able to do *independently*? How might the child participate more *independently*?
- How is the child *interacting* with others? How else could the child be *interacting*?
- How is the child *coping* with the happenings around him/her? What is overstimulating to the child? What does the child seem to react less to than expected?

Table 4.1 summarizes specific areas to look at within these big assessment questions.

Table 4.1 Specific Assessment Areas of Child Learning and Development

Area	Description
Developmental Domains	Cognition, communication, motor, social-emotional, and adaptive skills are naturally assessed as they are used to learn and participate. For example, while the family's goals for Franco center around eating and socializing, his motor needs are assessed when he has a hard time keeping his balance while sitting at child care.
Form vs. Function	Form is how a child expresses a developmental competence, while function is the actual competence expected.† The child looking at the pictures named in a book versus pointing to the picture are two forms of showing the same function—knowing the names of objects in pictures.
Quality	It's not only important to know what the child can do, but *how well* the child can do it. For example, a child may be able to walk, but his gait is a concern. Or, a child may only put two words together, but she has a lot of two-word phrases and continues to create new ones.
Generalization	The child uses competencies across different settings and with different people and objects. Therefore, competencies are assessed across multiple routine activities rather than just once or in one setting.‡

† Wolery, 2004; ‡ Meisels & Atkins-Burnett, 2000

A specific area that warrants elaboration is assessing a child's strengths. While families enter early intervention because of what the child is *not* doing, or the risk of not being able to do something, it is important to understand what the child *can* do—the child's current competencies, responses, and interests. These strengths can be used as a starting point for promoting further development.[18] For example, Jia's strength in signaling when she's overwhelmed is important to know so that when developmental challenges become too much, her family can read and respond to her signal and give her a break. Just as all domains work in concert to express a child's functioning, so too do a child's strengths and needs.

Assessments must consider a child's learning and development within the family culture. For example, is a child not initiating a conversation because she cannot, or because in her family children do not initiate conversation? Is a child still using a bottle because the family does not believe the child needs to use a cup yet? Or, has the family tried to teach the child to use a cup, but without success? Or, has the child not had an opportunity to use a cup because the family is unsure how best to teach this skill? If the family does not believe the child needs to be using a cup yet and that's why the child is not using a cup, one cannot conclude that the child *cannot* use the cup. Developmental strengths and needs are further understood when they are looked at in the context of his or her family.

Important People and Particular Places

Let's look back at how Franco learns and participates while eating at home and at child care. At home, his high chair provides the physical support he needs for stability in sitting. At child care, his chair does not provide this support, so he uses a lot of energy trying to stay on the chair. At home, he gets to practice using a spoon, while at child care he eats snacks with his fingers, so he doesn't have an opportunity to practice.[19] At home, Franco is focused on using the spoon, because it is quiet. However, the interaction is limited to him and his father. At child care, he has a lot of friends to interact with, who are also great models for learning eating skills. The excitement of these friends, however, makes it hard for him to focus on eating and he sometimes misses his mouth. This shows that children function very differently in different places. The characteristics of the routine activities—the places where children are—influence what a child learns and how a child participates. Therefore, assessments must look at the characteristics of the *environment*.

The important people in a routine activity—those who interact with the child—make up the *social environment* that influences child development. For example, Jia's mother allows Jia to take a break and come back to the interaction when she's ready. This interaction allows her to learn how to cope. The characteristics of objects, such as toys, tools, and furniture, the layout, and the sights and sounds of the routine activity make up the *physical environment*. The different chairs Franco sat in and the types of food are characteristics of the physical environment of snack time.

These environmental characteristics can be purposeful, such as conscious decisions on the family's part or specific intervention strategies. A parent might buy a blow-up ring seat so their infant has the hip support to sit and play (physical environment). Or, an intervention professional might suggest that the parent wait until the child asks to "go" before pulling the child in a wagon (social environment). Environmental characteristics can also be by chance; it just happens to be the way the environment occurs. For example, a family has a small living room with a lot of furniture, which easily allows the child to practice walking while holding on to furniture (physical environment). Or, when Franco is in child care he has models for eating (social environment). Early intervention professionals try to understand how the social and physical environment impacts child learning and development.[20] Knowing that, the early intervention partnership can enhance the positive aspects of the environment. For example, the family–professional partnership might identify strategies to further develop Franco's interactions with his friends. They can also identify ways to change those environmental aspects that make it hard for the child to learn. For example, Kevin and Franco's child care teacher chose a better chair for Franco to use. It is important to note that the early intervention team is not "evaluating" the environment as positive or negative overall, but its relationship to the child's unique learning characteristics. The early intervention partnership is looking for the fit between the child and the environment, with the goal of helping the child participate the best way he or she can.

When looking at how people interact with the child and how particular places are designed, the overarching question is, "What makes it challenging or easy for the child to learn, develop, and express his competencies?" These aspects were discussed in Chapter 2 as ways that children learn, and include opportunities to practice and participate in routine activities, creating the just right challenge, using the child's strengths, and interacting responsively. By understanding the social and physical environment, the family–professional partnership can identify potential strategies to further enhance child participation, learning, and development.

Strategies Tried and New

By looking at the characteristics of the environment that make up routine activities, the early intervention partnership can see how families and other adults in the child's life are supporting the child's development. These important strategies are already being used. Jia's mother is using responsive interactions to read her child's cues and wait for her to be ready to interact. Franco's father is making eating less of a challenge by holding the bowl steady for Franco. Sometimes, families do not know all the important strategies they are using to help their child learn.[21] They simply think of it as part of parenting. Early intervention professionals can help families identify all the great strategies they are already using, and build on them.

Families might have also previously tried strategies that didn't work. For example, as the Liangs try to help Jia learn to drink from a bottle, they might have tried a variety of nipples, different positions as she drinks, and different kinds of formula. The family identifies what has and has not worked so the family–professional partnership has all the information needed to identify potentially effective strategies.[22]

As a clear picture unfolds of the child's learning and development in routine activities, and the impact of the social and physical environment, potential strategies to enhance child development begin to emerge. When this happens, the assessment can be a time to try out potential strategies to see what happens.[23] This occurred when Kevin and Franco's child care teacher tried a different chair and found that Franco's stability improved. By testing strategies, the early intervention partnership sees, or assesses, how the child responds to the strategies, what the family and other important adults think of the strategies, and whether the strategies have the potential to be effective. These strategies should be comfortable for the important adults involved in the routine activities, and should fit seamlessly into the routine activity. For example, Kevin and Franco's child care teacher might discuss the possibility of having a snack that requires a spoon to eat and how that might work given the number of children in the classroom.

THE FAMILY–PROFESSIONAL PARTNERSHIP: COLLABORATION AND CONVERGENCE

Just like all aspects of early intervention, collaboration among the family–professional partnership is essential for successful assessments. The family brings to the partnership knowledge of their child: how their child participates in many routine activities, and how their child might respond to different strategies.[24] They can describe their child's behaviors in many different routine activities. The family also brings a history to the assessment—previous medical and developmental experiences—that might shed light on the child's learning characteristics. Families interpret child behaviors, as Jia's mother did in reading her child's behavior as needing a rest. Early intervention professionals also see how a child learns and participates in routine activities, but they will most likely see fewer routine activities than the family. Professionals interpret a child's behaviors based on knowledge of typical development, or what's expected at different ages, and how a child's development is unique. They also know how different areas of development impact each other. Armed with these strengths, the family–professional partnership collaborates to plan and implement the assessment, and interpret the assessment information.

All members of the family–professional partnership plan what the assessment will look like. The following questions are considered in the planning process:

- What is the focus of the assessment? What are the family's priorities and the reason behind the assessment? Are there any assessment requirements, such as scores on a particular instrument to determine eligibility?

- When and where should the assessment take place? During what routine activities does the family feel comfortable describing their observations? What routine activities does the family prefer the professional observes? What routine activities does the professional want to observe?
- Who should participate in the assessment? How should each member of the assessment team participate?

The family–professional partnership discusses the various ways family members and early intervention professionals can participate in the assessment and decide on each partners' responsibilities.[25] For example, when observing routine activities, a truly authentic picture of how the child learns and participates is only discovered if family members who are usually part of the routine activity participate as they normally do.[26] For example, Roberto interacts with Franco as he usually does so that Kevin can see how lunch time goes at home. Other family members who are participating in the assessment but are not usually part of the routine activity can observe along with early intervention professionals. The early intervention partnership notes: 1.) the child's competencies—what he has mastered, is learning to master, or is not yet learning; 2.) how the important people and particular places are helping the child learn; and 3.) potential strategies to further enhance the learning opportunities occurring in routine activities. By allowing real life to unfold, the early intervention partnership can be assured that they are obtaining an accurate developmental picture of the child.[27]

Other roles family members may choose to take on during the assessment process might be discussed. Family members, if they feel comfortable, can administer items on an instrument, which creates a more natural interaction for the child. Or, family members can watch how the child responds to an early intervention professional administering the items, noting the differences in the child in this situation and in typical routine activities.

All members of the early intervention partnership implement the assessment as decided during the planning phase. The early intervention partnership members are observing, talking about their observations, and testing potential strategies. While this information is being collected, each team member discusses his or her interpretations of what the information means in terms of the child's learning and development. All viewpoints are respected, and no one perspective is more important than another.

All the assessment information is gathered, and a clear picture of the child's learning characteristics and current developmental strengths and needs is created. It's okay if professionals and families have different views. It's also okay if family members disagree or professionals disagree. These many perspectives are the reason for having various team members. Through conversation and collaboration, the family–professional partnership pools the information and perspectives.[28] This process of *converging* perspectives results in a richer picture of the child's learning and development, recognizing how complex child development really is.[29]

Throughout the assessment process, the focus is to gather information and decide what that information means.

THE BIG PICTURE: RELATED POLICIES AND GUIDELINES

Early intervention guidelines that come from the federal government and early childhood associations outline important practices around how assessments are conducted so that accurate results and meaningful information is gathered. The Division for Early Childhood of the Council for Exceptional Children recommends that all assessments:

- occur through family and professional collaboration;
- are individualized;
- result in helpful information; and
- meet the guidelines of early intervention policies and professional associations.[30]

Federal early intervention regulations use different terms when assessment is used to determine eligibility versus when assessment is used for any other reason.[31] When eligibility is being determined, the assessment is called *evaluation*. The continuous process that occurs in early intervention once a family is eligible is called *assessment*. This process is used to understand "the child's unique strengths and needs and the services appropriate to meet those needs."[32] While these two terms are used, there is only one difference between evaluation and assessment. The difference is that, for evaluations, there must be at least two professionals from different disciplines participating in the eligibility process.[33] Each discipline brings a different perspective to share in the eligibility decision.

Despite the different terms, other regulations pertain to both evaluations and assessments. These regulations include *what* to assess and *how* to assess.[34] In general, the regulations state that evaluations and assessments have to gather a variety of information, including the child's health status, which may impact the course of his or her learning and development. While the regulations identify that each developmental domain needs to be assessed, it also states that those domains are assessed around child *functioning* or how the child uses those domains. There are two primary requirements on how to conduct evaluations and assessments. First, early intervention professionals must be trained to conduct assessments and second, *informed clinical opinion* must be used. Informed clinical opinion means that the family–professional partnership uses all the information collected through multiple methods (that is, observations, tools, different routine activities), rather than relying on one assessment tool or approach.[35] This is especially important in determining eligibility because of the important decision being made—whether a family will be able to participate in early intervention or not. The National Association for the Education of Young

Children (NAEYC) echoed this: "Decisions that have a major impact on children, such as enrollment or placement, are never made on the basis of results from a single developmental assessment . . . but are based on multiple sources of relevant information, including that obtained from observations of and interactions with children by teachers and parents."[36] In order to make sure that assessment methods are fair for all families, regardless of the family's culture or first language, early intervention regulations outline requirements for testing in the family's native language and using culturally appropriate tools and methods.

In addition to the federal regulations, the federal office responsible for the Part C Early Intervention program—the Office of Special Education Programs (OSEP) in the U.S. Department of Education—requires every state early intervention program to report on the developmental progress of early intervention participants on three functional outcomes. These outcomes are:

- positive social-emotional skills (including social relationships);
- acquisition and use of knowledge and skills (including early language/communication); and
- use of appropriate behavior to meet needs.[37]

These outcomes are another reason why children might be assessed—to determine the effectiveness of the early intervention program.[38] For each of these outcomes, the family–professional partnership determines if a child is making progress toward, or is functioning at a level typically expected for the child's age. Multiple sources of assessment information are gathered from early intervention partnership members, including observations, early intervention records, and results on assessment instruments. The observations and intervention records provide information about child functioning in routine activities and generalization of those skills across routine activities.[39] Results on assessment instruments are used to compare each child's development to what is typically expected for the child's age. There is one problem with using current assessment instruments. The results from most instruments are not divided into the three functional outcomes. Instead, they are usually separated into the traditional developmental domains. So, the information from assessment instruments needs to be converted into the functional outcomes. The ECO Center has done this conversion, known as *crosswalking*, to make the information from instruments more functional.

SUMMARY:
THE CHILD, IMPORTANT PEOPLE, AND PARTICULAR PLACES

Assessments are used to learn more about what a child's behaviors mean, his or her strengths and needs, and how best to support learning and development. A comprehensive picture of a child's development emerges when assessments are tailored to the unique family culture in which the child lives, learns, and grows. With this information, a plan can be made to determine the next steps in supporting child development based on the unique characteristics of the family and their vision and priorities.

Preparing for the Partnership: What Families Bring

The following questions can be considered by families as they prepare for participation in assessments:

Family Vision and Priorities:

What is important to you and your family? What is unique about your family?
What do you envision for your child as a member of your family?
What do you want your child to learn or be able to do?
What routine activities do you see as important learning opportunities?

Planning the Assessment:

What do you see as the reason for the assessment?
What questions do you have about the assessment?
What questions or reservations do you have about being observed while you
　　participate in routine activities?

Assessment Information:

How do you see your child participating in different routine activities?
Why do you think your child participates that way?
How would you describe your child's strengths and needs?
How does your child learn?
What do you do to help your child learn and participate in everyday life?

Preparing for the Partnership: What Professionals Bring

The following questions can be considered by early intervention professionals as they prepare for participation in assessments:

Family Vision and Priorities:

What do you already know about the family's priorities?
How will you guide the family in identifying their priorities? What tools will
　　you use?

Planning the Assessment:

What is required of the assessment according to your program's policies and
　　procedures?

What needs to be planned? How will you guide the planning process?
How will you explain why families are observed as they participate in routine
　activities?

Assessment Information:

How will you assess, or come to understand, the child's learning and
　development in routine activities?
How and what will you observe?
How will you gather the observations of other team members, including the
　family?
What questions will you ask?
What do you need to feel comfortable and competent in assessing:
 • functional competencies across domains?
 • the influence of the important people and particular places on child
　development?
What do you need to feel comfortable and competent in uncovering the
　strategies that:
 • are already being used?
 • have already been tried?
 • could be tried?

Chapter 5

WHAT AND WHY, WHERE AND WHEN, WHO AND HOW: PLANNING EARLY INTERVENTION SUPPORTS

The Coles-Williams family is participating in early intervention because of Dionne's developmental delays. Holly, the service coordinator partnering with the family, scheduled a meeting to decide what the family's early intervention program will look like. Of course, Dionne's parents, Kenisha Coles and Gary Williams, are at the meeting. Gary's mother is also there. She moved in with Kenisha and Gary to help care for Dionne after she was born. Sarah, an infant–toddler specialist, and Vicky, a physical therapist, were also there because they participated in the developmental assessment.

As discussed at the beginning of Chapter 4, each early intervention family–professional partnership crafts their own recipe for how best to meet family priorities. The ingredients are the family's vision and priorities for their child and their entire family, as well as the child and family's strengths and needs. Using this information, the family–professional partnership creates a plan that addresses the family's priorities in a way that is meaningful and fits the family. An initial plan is created when the family enters early intervention. This plan is regularly reviewed and updated as needed throughout the early intervention process. To create an intervention plan, the family–professional partnership focuses on two questions:

1. Given the child's learning characteristics, what is the best way to help the child meet the developmental outcomes desired by the family?
2. What can early intervention do so the family can help their child learn?

These questions outline the intervention plan. Specifically, the family–professional partnership plans: 1.) what the family–professional partnership wants to achieve and why; 2.) where and when early intervention supports are provided; and 3.) who makes up the family–professional partnership and how they will carry out the plan.

EXPECTED OUTCOMES: WHAT AND WHY

> During the intervention planning meeting, the family–professional partnership reviewed the family's priorities. Learning and independence are important to the Coles-Williams family. Therefore, they would like Dionne to explore things, such as toys and other objects in her routine activities, to learn and have fun. They would like her to be able to move around so she can get where she wants to on her own. Also, they want Dionne to eat more, as she currently gets most of her nutrition from a feeding tube. Because Dionne is now more medically stable, Gary's mother is hoping to move back to her own home. She will still care for Dionne on occasion, but Kenisha and Gary would like to find a weekday child care program that understands Dionne's care and developmental needs. These priorities are the focus of all planning decisions.

The intervention plan is known as the *road map* for the family–professional partnership.[1] Just like mapping out a trip, planning begins by identifying the starting point, where the family and child are now—and the end point—where the family wants to go. These starting and end points have already begun to be identified through the family conversations and developmental assessments described in Chapters 3 and 4. The family–professional partnership understands the family's values, priorities, and vision—where they want to go. They also know where they are now. They know how the child is currently learning and participating in routine activities, and how the people, materials, and setting of the routine activities affect how the child learns and participates. They know how the family is working toward meeting the priorities of individual family members, and the family as a whole. For each priority of the family, specific outcomes are created.

One might think, aren't the outcomes the same as the family's visions and priorities? Well, yes and no. Every family priority is represented in an outcome.[2] However, family priorities can be broader and longer term than early intervention outcomes. For example, the family's priorities of Dionne learning, having fun, getting places on her own, and eating can be important priorities throughout her childhood. When she is a preschooler, she might have fun by playing group games with other children her own age. When she is in elementary school, learning might center on academic school work. When she is a teenager, getting to places on her own might be driving or taking public transportation. Whether she is eating on her own or through a tube, Dionne's family will most likely think about her nutritional needs. And, as all families do, Dionne's family will make sure that any child care programs, schools, or community activities that Dionne participates in are a good match for Dionne.

Chapter 4 identified ways to create outcomes from the family's broader priorities. These included questions such as, "What might that look like in the near future?" Priorities are the family's overarching values and goals. Outcomes are the expected early intervention accomplishments related to those priorities. These outcomes are individualized to the child's unique learning characteristics and reflect the everyday competencies needed to learn and participate in routine activities.[3] Selected outcomes created by the Coles-Williams family–professional partnership are illustrated in Table 5.1. Each outcome specifies what will be achieved and how that achievement is related to the family's priorities.[4] The part of each outcome representing the family's priorities is in italics.

Table 5.1. Selected Outcomes, Steps, and Approaches to Meet the Coles-Williamses' Priorities

Outcome†	Steps	Approaches
Dionne will explore objects by touching, shaking, and banging them *to learn and have fun* Routine Activities: • Playtime throughout the day • Eating • Diaper changing	1. Dionne will hold objects and look at objects when placed in her hand until she's no longer interested in them. 2. Dionne will imitate touching, shaking, and banging objects by taking 4 turns of back and forth imitation. 3. Dionne will touch, shake, and bang objects on her own for 3 minutes.	Use objects that make sound since Dionne likes them. Dionne plays best sitting in her baby seat. Use objects that Dionne can get her whole hand around. Let Dionne say when she's ready to play or done playing. Show Dionne different ways to explore objects. Assist her as needed. See if Dionne will initiate turn-taking.
Dionne will move around her house *to get things and go places she wants to go on her own.* Routine Activities: • Playtime on the floor and on the bed	1. Dionne will play on her stomach by looking at toys and interacting face to face with her family until she is tired of the activity. 2. Dionne will roll onto her stomach and onto her back to get toys and move toward a family member.	Put a rolled towel under her shoulders to help her prop up on her stomach. Be face to face with Dionne when on her stomach so she can interact with you. Put favorite toys a little out of reach. Use toys that make noise to get her attention. Help her roll by putting her on her side to get something.
The Coles-Williams family will have quality child care *so Dionne is cared for and learning while her parents are at work.*	1. Holly will look into child care programs close to the parents' work that have experience with children with disabilities and special health care needs. 2. Kenisha, Gary, and Holly will visit possible child care options. 3. Kenisha and Gary will apply to the program(s) that best meet their interests.	Identify the qualities of child care important to the family. List important questions to ask before visiting programs. Discuss the importance of collaborating with the professionals involved with Dionne, including early intervention and her medical providers, and the expected responsibilities of the child care program.

† All outcomes are achieved when the family is satisfied that they have been met.

Checkpoints Along the Way

Outcomes are the expected achievements down the road. To make sure the family–professional partnership is on the right track and progressing toward meeting the outcomes, the family–professional partnership identifies *checkpoints*, or steps along the way to achieve the outcomes. These steps are also called *objectives*. The steps, or objectives, for the Coles-Williamses' outcomes are described in Table 5.1. Even if an outcome takes a long time to achieve, the steps provide a way to identify what it takes to achieve the outcome, and how the family–professional partnership is progressing toward it.

Each step describes specifically what the outcome will look like when it's achieved and how the family–professional partnership will know when the competency is mastered. Mastery is sometimes described as a certain amount of time (for example, 3 minutes), level of completion (for example, half a bowl of cereal or the whole bowl), the number of times (for example, four back and forth turn-taking exchanges), or when the child is no longer interested. Sometimes, mastery is defined as when the family is satisfied that the outcome or step has been achieved.[5] This is how the Coles-Williams family–professional partnership will know the outcomes are achieved (see the asterisk in Table 5.1). Note in Table 5.1 that both child and family outcomes have steps to achieve the outcome.

Sometimes, professionals rely on the family to identify the steps to meeting outcomes. A professional might feel that, since the outcome is the family's to identify, the family should identify the steps as well. While some families can identify those steps, families are not necessarily familiar with how development unfolds, especially for children with developmental delays or disabilities. The family–professional partnership collaborates to identify the steps that make sense for the particular child, with the particular family, and in the particular family culture and routine activities.[6]

Approaches to Use

As described in Chapters 3 and 4, the family–professional partnership comes to understand the child's unique learning characteristics—how the child learns best, strengths to build on, and needs to address. The partnership knows how the people and materials in the routine activities support the child's learning, has tried out strategies to see if they work, and knows the strategies already tried. They also know the ways the family tries to attain their priorities. From this, the family–professional partnership identifies specific approaches to meet the family's outcomes for their child and their family.

These approaches can be specific learning strategies to promote child development—ways to interact with the child and materials to use—such as those listed for Dionne's outcomes. Approaches may also be ways to meet family outcomes, like those listed in Table 5.1, so that Kenisha and Gary can find child care. Approaches can also describe the way the family–professional partnership will collaborate. These approaches are described in Chapter 6. The family–professional partnership collaborates to ensure that the approaches taken fit the family,[7] are based on research,[8] and, for child outcomes, promote developmental strengths and address developmental needs across domains. Approaches are described in the intervention plan, and then refined during intervention visits.

In Chapter 2, we discussed how children participate and learn in routine activities by using their competencies across developmental domains. The child's strengths and needs in each domain contribute to how they learn and participate in routine activities. Since outcomes describe how the child is expected to participate in routine activities, outcomes also span developmental domains. To best address outcomes, the family–professional partnership identifies learning strategies across all developmental domains—strategies that build on the child's strengths and address the child's needs. Let's look at the strategies suggested for Dionne's outcome of exploring objects and the related domains:

- showing her ways to explore through touching, shaking, and banging toys (cognitive);
- building off her interest in toys that make noise (social-emotional);
- taking turns in the back and forth imitation to initiate and respond to another (social communication);
- making sure she is positioned in a way that makes it easy for her to use her hands (gross motor);
- identifying the easiest toys for her to hold onto, while also promoting her to reach and grasp (fine motor); and
- responding to her ways of communicating when she wants to play and when she is done playing (communication).

When all domains are attended to, interventions are designed the way children learn and participate, by using all domains at the same time.

Some approaches are the ways family members can interact with Dionne to promote learning. Other approaches are materials that can help Dionne learn. A specific kind of material is called *assistive technology*, or AT. AT is any material that is changed or added to a routine activity that helps a child participate and learn. For example, using a rolled towel to help Dionne prop up on her stomach is considered AT. Assistive technology can also include more sophisticated products, such as electronic communication devices that "talk" for the child, or equipment that helps children sit, stand, or move around.[9] While everyday intervention professionals come with knowledge of AT, there are also experts in AT options. For example, the Coles-Williams family–professional partnership decides to have an AT evaluation to determine if there are better seating options for Dionne.

Note in Table 5.1 that outcomes, steps, and approaches can span routine activities to provide multiple opportunities for practice. Sometimes, like Dionne's outcome on eating (not shown in Table 5.1), the outcomes, steps, and approaches would be specific to one routine activity. While this outcome is only during one routine activity, eating occurs many times throughout the day, providing multiple opportunities to practice. After the outcomes, steps, and approaches are identified, the way the family and early intervention professionals will collaborate can be planned.

FAMILY–PROFESSIONAL COLLABORATION: WHERE AND WHEN

By reviewing the outcomes, steps, and approaches, the Coles-Williams family–professional partnership identified where and how often interventions should occur. They decided that—based on the outcomes—the intervention visits should occur during the routine activities of meal times and playtimes, and that the intervention professional(s) should come at times when Gary and Kenisha are home from work, as well as when Gary's mother is caring for Dionne. Given this, and that the approaches identified are all new for the family, the family–professional partnership decided that intervention visits should occur 3 times a week until the family feels comfortable with the strategies. At that point, the partnership can evaluate whether three visits a week continue to be needed.

In the previous section, the outcomes and steps to be achieved, and the approaches to get there, were identified. These ultimately are the family's to use as a guide to meeting their priorities. In some programs outside of early intervention, supports stop there, with periodic follow up. For example, a doctor might provide an approach (that is, strategies) the family can use at home to alleviate a child's cold. A developmental specialist at a children's hospital might conduct a developmental assessment and provide ways (that is, approaches) the family can help their child learn at home. This support can work for some families and with children with certain learning characteristics. However, the unique learning styles of children with developmental delays or disabilities could call for more ongoing support for families. What this support looks like is individualized for each family. Just like the doctor and developmental specialist, the early intervention professional is there to support the family as they promote their child's development and address their family and parenting priorities. The family–professional partnership determines suitable early intervention supports by answering, "What supports can help the family meet their outcomes?" This results in the identification of *where* interventions will occur and *when* interventions will occur.

Where Interventions Occur: Routine Activities

Where should the family–professional partnership collaborate to meet intervention outcomes? According to the Individuals with Disabilities Education Act (IDEA), the response is the child's natural environment. The definition of natural environment is a place—home, community, or classroom where "children without disabilities participate."[10] As stated in Chapter 2, however, these locations are not enough to define the learning opportunities available in everyday life.[11] Instead, early intervention leadership focuses on the routine activities in which the child participates, considering the people, materials, and ways the routine activities occur.[12] These are the times when families will use the strategies to facilitate child learning and development in between intervention visits.[13] Therefore, intervention visits occur during those same routine activities. For the Coles-Williams family, these are mealtimes and playtimes; with Dionne's parents some of the time and her grandmother other times. For the Carmina family from previous chapters, intervention visits occurred during morning "hang out" time with and without Charlie's siblings, getting ready for bed, and swimming class.

Sometimes, interventions to address child outcomes may only occur at child care, since a child spends a large portion of the day there. While this might be agreed upon by the family–professional partnership, it is not assumed that this is the only time early intervention supports can occur. For example, while Aiden and Elliot in Chapter 3 go to child care everyday, the Simmons-Crause family still wants to help the boys learn when they are with their family, in the evenings and on the weekends. Therefore, for this family, intervention visits occur during specific child care activities *and* at home. The family–professional partnership collaborates to determine where supports will best be provided so that all adults are able to promote child learning and development.

When Interventions Occur (How Often)

How often should intervention visits occur? Currently, research provides little guidance on this topic. Therefore, it is up to the family–professional partnership to determine the most appropriate level of support for the individual family. Intervention visits are a time for the family–professional partnership to ensure that the family feels comfortable and able to use the learning strategies in between intervention visits (see Chapter 6).[14] They are also a time to address family and parenting outcomes. The overarching answer to the "how often" question is—often enough that the family feels supported in making decisions and using the approaches to meet their outcomes.[15] Therefore, visits occur frequently enough so that the family–professional partnership can problem solve strategies and partner around the early intervention outcomes. If visits occur too infrequently, the family may have questions, need more guidance, or want more strategies sooner than when the next intervention visit occurs. Making too many visits, however, can have its drawbacks as well. First, if the intervention professional visits too often, the family might feel like they *need* the intervention professional there, and feel less confident in their own strengths and abilities.[16] If the strategies and approaches are working well for the family, visits can be less frequent as less support is needed. There is something to be said for checking in to make sure the approaches continue to work for the family. However, these visits could occur less frequently than if new strategies or approaches were introduced. Identifying the frequency of intervention visits requires the family–professional partnership to envision the level of support the family will need to use the intervention approaches on their own. To identify the just-right number of visits, the family–professional partnership can ask:

Is this a new strategy? Families will most likely want more frequent support when they are learning a new strategy.

How complex is the strategy for the family? All strategies should be doable for the family, but some strategies are more complex than others.[17] All members of the family–professional partnership share their perspectives on how complex they feel the strategy is. More complex strategies may call for more frequent visits.

How comfortable is the family with the strategies?[18] If a family is unsure about a strategy, or how they are using a strategy, the family–professional partnership might decide to meet more frequently. During these visits, either the family becomes comfortable with the strategy or the partnership can change the strategy (see Chapter 6).

How quickly will the strategy change? Some children will develop at a faster rate than others. As children progress, new strategies might be needed to promote new competencies. The more frequently the strategies are expected to change, the more frequently visits can be scheduled.[19]

What is the family's learning style? Some families will want more specific, or concrete, supports when learning to use intervention strategies. Other families may feel they can use recommended strategies with less support. When families receive support they feel they do not need, their confidence and competence in parenting can be negatively affected.[20] Therefore, the family's desired level of support is considered when determining frequency.

The frequency of intervention visits is not set in stone. If intervention visits feel like they are occurring too often or not often enough, the family–professional partnership can collaborate to decide on a new frequency. The family brings knowledge of how they learn and, given the strategies, their support needs. The professionals come with knowledge about strategies in general and how much support is required to learn the strategies, based on their previous experiences. Together, the family–professional partnership can decide on the just-right frequency of support.

FAMILY–PROFESSIONAL PARTNERSHIP PROCESS:
WHO AND HOW

During the planning meeting for the Coles-Williams family, the meeting participants identified the partnership members who will be responsible for carrying out the intervention plan. Of course, Dionne's parents will be responsible, as well as Holly, the service coordinator. Because Dionne's grandmother is an integral part of the Dionne's life and regularly cares for her, she wants to participate so she can best support Dionne's learning and development. The family–professional partnership decided that Sarah, the special instructor who participated in the developmental assessment, will be the professional who is the constant in intervention visits. Sarah will integrate the strategies and recommendations across domains for each outcome. Sarah suggests that, due to Dionne's learning characteristics, a professional with expertise in motor and eating could be an important partnership member. Sarah and this person can come on intervention visits together, since both will be working on the same outcomes. Vicky, the physical therapist at the meeting, recommends that Julio be this person. He is an occupational therapist with a lot of knowledge of motor development for young children, and specializes in eating. The family–professional partnership decides that Julio will come with Sarah for one of the 3 weekly visits. Sarah can continue to work with the family on all outcomes the other 2 visits. Julio, however, will be available to come other times if needed. In addition, Regina, a vision specialist who regularly works with Sarah and Julio's intervention team, will join the family–professional partnership. Regina will come with Sarah once a month on an intervention visit to check in and provide supports to both Sarah and the Coles-Williams family.

At the heart of all early intervention processes is the family–professional partnership. But who makes up the partnership? How will partnership members collaborate to carry out the plan?

Identifying the Family–Professional Partnership

Who comprises the family–professional partnership is decided on an individual basis.[21] All partnerships, of course, include the child's parent(s) or legal guardian(s). Every partnership also has a professional, like Holly, who is responsible for carrying out service coordination tasks (see Chapter 8). Additional family members might be included, such as Dionne's grandmother. Community members may also join the family–professional partnership. For example, Elliot and Aiden's child care teacher from Chapter 3 wants to know how to promote learning and development during child care activities and would welcome support from early intervention professionals. Charlie Carmina's swimming teacher was also a partnership member since intervention visits occurred during those classes.

In addition to family and community members, early intervention professionals join the family–professional partnership. These professionals may or may not be a part of the initial planning meeting, as the actual partnership members are not known until the planning meeting. That is why Vicky, who knows the family from the developmental assessment, is participating. When a plan is updated and revised, different professionals than those already in the partnership might be added or substituted.

There are a variety of early intervention professionals, with different disciplinary expertise, who are available to support families in meeting their early intervention outcomes. The four most frequent professional disciplines are:

1. *Occupational Therapists*, who have expertise in fine motor and sensory development;
2. *Physical Therapists*, who have expertise in gross motor development, including movement and positioning;
3. *Special Instructors* (known by different names in different early intervention programs, including special educators, developmental therapists, and infant–toddler specialists), who have expertise in child learning and development, and most particularly cognitive, social-emotional, behavioral, and play development; and
4. *Speech Language Pathologists/Speech Therapists*, who have expertise in communication and oral motor (that is, how the muscles in the mouth are used) development.

While these professionals have their areas of expertise, every professional is responsible for 1.) understanding and promoting learning and development across domains, 2.) working in routine activities, and 3.) knowing how to share their knowledge and expertise with family–professional partnership members.[22] That is why Sarah, the infant–toddler specialist, can address all the outcomes on the intervention plan, with support from Julio and Regina.

It was once thought that outcomes could be divided into different developmental domains. And, if there was a speech outcome—an outcome that focused on communication—then a speech pathologist would join the partnership. However, recall earlier that all outcomes span developmental domains. So, no outcome belongs to one professional.[23] Instead, when choosing who should be a part of the family–professional partnership, the overarching question is: "Who can best support the family in meeting their early intervention outcomes?" To answer this question, the family–professional partnership considers both expertise and fit.[24]

Sarah was chosen to be the main professional to work with the Coles-Williams family because she has an expertise in play and promoting independence and learning, important priorities of the Coles-Williams family. Expertise is also needed in eating, motor, and visual development. To address eating and motor development, not just any professional, or professionals, were chosen. Instead, Julio was specifically identified, because he could provide expertise in two areas, eating and motor. That way, the number of professionals on the team is reduced, but the expertise is still there. Regina, the vision specialist, was also purposely chosen. This decision was both for her understanding of visual development and because her existing relationship with Julio and Sarah makes it easier to work together.

Fit also considers the availability of the specific professional.[25] Since intervention visits occur during the routine activities where families will use the strategies, the chosen professional needs to be available to visit when the routine activities usually occur. For example, Patrice prefers to start her day later in the morning and work into the evening. The Carmina family would like support during the bedtime routine. Therefore, the combination of Patrice's expertise and her working hours made her a perfect fit for the Carmina's family–professional partnership.

Ways of Partnering

Once the members of the family–professional partnership are identified, they decide how to partner with each other. Traditionally, each early intervention professional in the partnership, representing different disciplines, worked separately with the family, attending to the developmental domain of their expertise.[26] Then, early intervention professionals began to coordinate their efforts. Each professional in the partnership addressed the same outcomes, and shared information with each other, but still focused on their domain of expertise or discipline.[27] There is very little research on the best ways for professionals to work together, or team. However, these ways of teaming make it difficult for any professional to fully address any outcome. What if Sarah only focused on how Dionne explored, but didn't include ways for her to say when she wanted to play? There would be a missed opportunity to promote her language development. Or, what if Sarah didn't position Dionne so she could best use her hands? Then, Dionne would not be able to explore as well as she could when supported. Or, what if Julio did not provide a goal, or purpose for Dionne to move? Dionne might learn how to move, but not know why she would want to. Each team member would be working separately leaving the family to pull it all together.[28] There needs to be a way to blend the expertise across the professional partnership members.

For over 10 years, some early intervention leaders have suggested a way for the family–professional partnership to work together.[29] In this way, all early intervention professionals work on all the early intervention outcomes, and attend to all domains, just like how children learn and participate. Since all domains are addressed together, there is no need for separate visits by different professionals. This way of working together is called *transdisciplinary* because professionals move beyond what is traditionally their own disciplinary expertise and address all developmental domains.[30] While some professionals are reluctant to use this model,[31] the transdisciplinary model is recommended by the Division for Early Childhood of the Council for Exceptional Children (DEC).[32]

The transdisciplinary model works the way children actually learn and, subsequently, outcomes are created. Namely, all professionals focus on all the developmental domains as the child functions in real life. One might think, if all early intervention professionals can do this, then why is there a need for different professionals? While all professionals are knowledgeable in child development overall and in how to promote learning and development, different professionals are still needed because they are the experts in their disciplines. However, what is different is *how* that expertise is used.[33] Instead of each professional working separately with a family, professionals share their expertise with professionals from other disciplines. These professionals do not become the other disciplines, but they do become even more competent professionals by utilizing knowledge across disciplines.[34] For example, Sarah and Julio will work together with the Coles-Williams family. Both Sarah and Julio will learn more about promoting child development when children have learning characteristics similar to Dionne's. Julio can learn more about what Sarah knows, and Sarah can learn more about what Julio knows. Because Sarah has a strong understanding of development in general, she can apply the new knowledge she learns from Julio with the Coles-Williams family when Julio is not visiting with her. Another example is Patrice, the physical therapist working with the Carmina family. Patrice has a lot of experience in child development across domains, and can help the Carminas support Charlie's development across all domains, without the direct support of another professional coming with her. The expected benefits of working this way are:

> *Interventions fit the way the child learns and participates in routine activities.* Namely, by focusing on and integrating strategies across developmental domains into functional competencies.
>
> *The family has only one set of recommendations.* A research study has found that the *more* early intervention professionals working with a family, the *less* satisfied families are with early intervention supports.[35] Instead of juggling multiple professionals and multiple recommendations, families have one set of recommended approaches that strengthen the child's strengths and meet the child's needs.[36]
>
> *The chance of duplicating supports is reduced.* If all professionals work on the same outcomes, using the same strategies, there would be no need for all the professionals to partner directly with the family. If they did, they would be saying the same thing and doing the same thing. Instead, the family partners directly with the fewest number of professionals who work together as one.[37]
>
> *Each discipline's professional expertise is still respected and utilized.*[38] The expertise all professionals bring to the family–professional partnership is

applied during the intervention visits with the family, just in a cohesive, rather than discrete, way.

So what does the transdisciplinary model look like? As mentioned above, the fewest number of professionals decided upon by the family–professional partnership, participates in the intervention visits with the family.[39] There is one early intervention professional who is the constant in visits, such as Sarah.[40] But, these early intervention professionals aren't alone in their work. Other professional members of the early intervention partnership are available to assist as needed. In other words, the family–professional partnership decides which early intervention professionals are going to work directly with the family, and which will provide consultation to the family and the intervention professionals who work directly with the family.

The family–professional partnership identifies the early intervention professionals who will provide *direct supports* to the family during intervention visits. There may be one professional with the family, the way Patrice partners with the Carmina family. Or, professionals might come together to the intervention visit, or co-visit, to support the family. Sarah directly supports the Coles-Williams family 3 times a week. Once a week, Julio co-visits with her. This way, interventions are blended into one, instead of two separate interventions.[41]

The family–professional partnership also identifies other early intervention professionals to provide indirect supports, through what is called, *consultation*.[42] These consulting professionals are there to provide their expertise as needed. The type of support provided by the consulting professionals depends on the family's priorities, the child's learning characteristics, and the direct professional's knowledge and experience.[43] For example, Patrice, the physical therapist partnering with the Carmina family, went to school not only for physical therapy, but also for early intervention specifically, learning about infant–toddler development across the domains and addressing the needs of infants and toddlers with developmental delays or disabilities. Based on the family's outcomes and Charlie's development, Patrice feels quite comfortable being the only professional directly partnering with the Carminas to address family priorities. However, even Patrice, with all her expertise, is not alone. Jessica, the developmental specialist, frequently consults with Patrice outside of intervention visits. Patrice and Jessica discuss how the intervention visits are going. Jessica provides ideas and information during these meetings that Patrice can take back to the Carminas during the intervention visits. If necessary, Jessica can go on a co-visit with Patrice if the family–professional partnership decides that would be helpful. Sarah also is well versed in child development and early intervention. Because the incidence of children with visual impairments is low, however, she has less experience with infants and toddlers with vision impairments. Therefore, Regina, a vision specialist, consults directly during the intervention visits with the Coles-Williams family. That way, Regina is providing the level of support Sarah and the Coles-Williams family need from a specialist to promote Dionne's learning and development.

When planning how the family–professional partnership members will carry out the plan, they think about the support needs of the family, child, and intervention professional.[44] All family–professional partnership members—providing direct supports or consultation—are responsible for creating the plan, carrying it out, and determining its effectiveness.[45] The different aspects of the intervention plan—what and why, where and when, and who and how—should make sense as a cohesive plan.

PURPOSEFUL PLANNING

Creating the early intervention plan is a very important part of the early intervention process. The intervention plan is not meant to be a bureaucratic form to be filled out. It is meant to identify *what* will occur during intervention visits and *how* interventions will occur. The family–professional partnership requires time and attention to create a plan that reflects the purpose and process of the interventions for the particular family. Families will understand how early intervention works because it is outlined in the plan.[46] Therefore, the family–professional partnership makes sure the plan is realistic and reflects what the family wants from early intervention. Collaboration among family and professional partners is essential to create a plan that will fit the family.

While there may be one meeting time when the plan is written down, planning begins prior to the meeting, and continues throughout early intervention. Planning starts when priorities are identified early on and developmental assessments occur. The family–professional partnership uses prior conversations and observations to create the plan. Even after the plan is created, it is frequently revisited to make sure: 1.) the outcomes are still valued by the family; 2.) progress toward the outcomes is happening; 3.) the strategies work for the family; and 4.) the team structure is successful. Remember, the plan is individualized for each family–professional partnership, so it might take some fine-tuning before the plan is just right. Plans are meant to be flexible in that they can be revised at any time based on what was learned since the previous plan.

The family–professional partnership openly discusses whether the plan fits the individual family. Both family and professional partnership members need to feel comfortable with the plan, and be able to honestly discuss what they think the plan should look like, and why. To do this, all members of the family–professional partnership need to fully participate in the planning process. The family–professional partnership can identify ways to make sure that happens. Some families may want other supports during planning, such as a friend or another parent who's been through early intervention.[47] Some families may benefit from a translator to make certain that families who speak a language other than that of the early intervention professionals can fully participate in the planning process.[48] Professionals can make sure that all families are able to collaboratively participate in intervention planning.

In summary, intervention plans:

- focus on what the family envisions for the family and child's development;
- support participation and functioning in home and community life;
- reflect the support needs that best fit the family's culture and way of life;
- are clear so all partners understand the plan; and
- are collaboratively designed by the family and professional partners.[49]

THE BIG PICTURE:
RELATED POLICIES AND GUIDELINES

The Individuals with Disabilities Act (IDEA) legislation[50] and regulations[51] provide specific guidance on creating intervention plans. In early intervention programs under the IDEA, this plan is called the Individualized Family Service Plan, or IFSP. IFSP meetings to create or revise the plan must be scheduled at a time and place that works for the family. To ensure family participation, the regulations further state that the meeting must occur "in the native language of the parents . . . unless clearly not feasible to do so."[52] At least every 6 months, the plan is reviewed to identify progress toward meeting the intervention outcomes.

The IFSP has required components to it, most of which have been described above. The IFSP summarizes the information collected through family conversations and developmental assessments. This summary includes the child's development and, if the family is interested in family or parenting outcomes, the family's concerns, priorities, and resources (see Chapter 3). Such documentation provides the information necessary for planning, starting with the "measurable results or outcomes expected to be achieved for the infant or toddler and the family."[53] Services, as best as possible, are based on "scientifically based research,"[54] and are defined by their "frequency, intensity and method of delivering services."[55] Additionally, the IFSP must include a statement about the other services families have, or could use, outside of early intervention. This way, the early intervention family–professional partnership can coordinate with those supports to make sure that *all* of the family's priorities are addressed (see Chapter 8). As described in Chapter 2, IDEA specifies the location of services as natural environments. It is during the IFSP meeting that the family–professional partnership identifies the natural environments where early intervention will occur or justifies why the child's outcomes cannot be achieved in natural environments.

The Division for Early Childhood of the Council for Exceptional Children's recommended practices provide guidance on how the family–professional partnership can best work together.[56] Many of these recommendations are described earlier. One overarching recommendation, however, is that professionals and family members work together, and share information with each other. That way, professionals understand the family and can provide information tailored to the family, and the family can make knowledgeable decisions about the supports and strategies for them.

Additionally, the American Academy of Pediatrics recommends that the child's pediatrician participate in the creation of the IFSP.[57] The doctor can contribute health information that is pertinent to early intervention supports, including information about the medical services the child receives from various health professionals (see Chapter 8).

SUMMARY: PLANNING INTERVENTION SUPPORTS

By planning early intervention supports, the family–professional partnership has an outline of what will be achieved, how it will be achieved, and who will be responsible for achieving it. That way, the family has the necessary support to help their child learn and develop within the routine activities of everyday life, according to the child's unique learning characteristics and the family's values and priorities.

Preparing for the Partnership: What Families Bring

Families can consider the following questions to prepare for planning early intervention supports:

What and Why

What questions do you have about outcomes? Based on your priorities, what outcomes do you want to achieve in early intervention?

What steps do you envision to achieve your outcomes? What questions do you have about possible steps?

What are approaches you have tried or are using to meet your priorities? What are some other approaches you might try?

What questions do you have for the family–professional partnership members about approaches to try?

Where and When

What questions do you have about natural environments? What routine activities do you see as places for intervention visits?

How frequently do you think you would like supports through intervention visits?

What is your learning style? What is hard for you to do? What is easy?

Who and How

Who in your family and community should be a part of the family–professional partnership?

What kind of support would you like from the early intervention professional(s) who directly support(s) you?

What do you think is important to consider when choosing the professional member(s) of the team?

What questions do you have about the transdisciplinary model?

Purposeful Planning

What supports (for example, friends or other contacts, translators) can help you fully participate in planning interventions?

How comfortable do you feel participating in intervention planning? How will you describe that to the family–professional partnership?

Preparing for the Partnership: What Professionals Bring

Professionals can consider the following questions to prepare for planning early intervention supports:

What and Why

How will you identify specific, functional outcomes from the family's priorities?

Based on the family's priorities and assessment information, do you have all the information needed to identify steps to achieve the outcome? What additional information do you need?

Based on the family's priorities and assessment information, what are some possible approaches to meeting the family's priorities? Who else do you need to speak to about possible approaches?

Where and When

How will you describe natural environments and routine activities? How will you support the family in identifying where interventions should occur?

How will you determine the just right frequency of intervention visits?

Who and How

How will you describe the transdisciplinary model? What else do you need to know about the model?

Who is available to be potential professional partnership members? In what capacity (direct providers, consultants)? What do you need to know about the partnership members (such as schedule, expertise, knowledge)?

Purposeful Planning

What do you know about the rules and regulations for creating an intervention plan (IFSP)? What else do you need to know?

How will you identify any supports (such as friends or other contacts, translators) the family could use when planning interventions? How will you obtain those supports?

Chapter 6

A PARTNERSHIP LEARNING TOGETHER

Picture this:

> The early intervention professional sits on the family's living room floor with her bag of toys she brought from her office. Across from her on the floor, the child sits in between his parent's legs. The professional uses the toys from her bag to teach the child different developmental skills, and tells the parent what she is trying to teach. The parent watches, motivates, and praises the child; soothes the child when he's upset; and listens as the professional describes how the parent could use the child's own toys and other objects to promote the same skills. At the end of the visit, the professional and parent schedule the next visit for the same day and the same time the following week. The professional packs up her toys and leaves.

Now picture this:

> The early intervention professional arrives at the family's home at the scheduled time, chosen because it was when playtime usually occurs. Playtime was specifically identified by the family as the routine activity in which the family wanted support helping their child learn. The professional watches as the parent and child play together with their everyday toys. The parent and professional discuss potential strategies that could promote the child's participation and learning, and identify which ones seem to best fit the family and routine activity. The family and professional feel some strategies are easy to do and simply discuss them. For other strategies, the professional shows the parent how to do them. Then, the parent tries out the strategies while the professional coaches the parent through it. Afterward, both parent and professional discuss how they felt about the strategies. The professional and parent schedule the next visit at a different day and time—when they are usually outside in the

backyard—to identify how the strategies could work in promoting the child's learning and development during that routine activity. The professional leaves the parent and child to continue with their day.

The first situation might be the way many think early intervention is supposed to work. After all, a client doesn't go to an accountant and expect to be shown how to do one's own taxes. A client doesn't expect a lawyer to tell the client how to try his own case. In both cases, the professional "does for" the client. But early intervention is not about this kind of relationship. Routine activities are full of opportunities for children to learn and develop. Families can and do use these opportunities to help their children learn. Early intervention does not have to, nor can it, take over that role. Early intervention professionals are not a part of the family's everyday life. Instead, they support families in promoting their child's learning based on their child's unique developmental characteristics. Together, during intervention visits, the early intervention professional and family decide on strategies that will help the child learn, grow, and participate in family life. During these visits, the family–professional partnership is assured that the family is comfortable with and able to use the strategies in between intervention visits, when the child is truly learning.[1]

During intervention visits, the family–professional partnership works like a coaching or consultative relationship. Consider the images that the words *coach* or *consultant* conjure up, whether it is a life coach, a coach of a sports team, or a management consultant for a corporation. This person helps the individual, team, or company meet the goals they've identified for themselves. The coach or consultant assesses what is currently happening and provides guidance on how to meet the goals, but expects the individual, team, or company to actually implement the strategies and achieve the goals. The time the family and professional have together—the intervention visits—is used for this same purpose. The professional's role is to support child learning by guiding the family in ways to help their child learn. At the same time, the early intervention professional is learning about the family, the best ways to work with them, and the strategies that best fit the family. With each successful collaboration, the professional learns more about being a coach and consultant.

While recommended practices endorse this coaching or consultation model, research has suggested that this is easier said than done.[2] Professionals are not always taught how to support families in promoting their child's development. More research is needed to fully understand what makes effective intervention visits. Practical guidance on what intervention visits should look like, however, has been clearly identified by early intervention leaders. These practices are based on what we know about how young children learn and develop, and how adults learn. The second example at the beginning of this chapter reflects these practices. Specifically, effective intervention visits:

- use the knowledge, skills, and abilities of all members of the family–professional partnership;

- occur in the family's everyday routine activities;
- apply strategies that encourage child engagement and participation; and
- promote family ability and confidence in effectively using strategies in between intervention visits.

By now, these concepts and the reasons for them are most likely familiar. In this chapter, these concepts are translated into specific practices to illustrate how they are used during intervention visits in the home.

FAMILY–PROFESSIONAL PARTNERSHIP: KEYS TO COLLABORATION

Just like other aspects of early intervention, the family–professional partnership is essential to successful intervention visits. A true, collaborative partnership invites families to fully participate in intervention visits so they can feel comfortable and be able to use effective learning strategies between visits. There are three building blocks to effective collaboration during intervention visits: 1.) identifying a common purpose; 2.) using family–professional strengths; and 3.) being flexible.

Common Purpose

Early intervention works differently from many professions. The differences are apparent not only in the accountant and lawyer examples described above, but also in the different way developmental professionals work in the home and community versus teachers in the classroom and therapists in hospitals, clinics, or office settings.[3] All members of the family–professional partnership need a clear understanding of this difference. The partnership discusses the role of early intervention—that early intervention is a support, not a substitute, for what families are already doing around parenting in general and promoting child development specifically. All family members and all professionals have to agree on what early intervention is about, not just those who most frequently partner. For example, even if Sarah comes to the home when Dionne's parents are there, does Gary's mother, who watches Dionne when her parents are at work, know what is expected of her when Sarah comes? Does Dionne's vision specialist who only sees the Coles-Williams family once a month, understand the purpose of early intervention? When there is open, honest communication, the entire family–professional partnership recognizes and works toward a common purpose.

Family–Professional Strengths

As discussed before, families bring knowledge of their child and family, and professionals bring knowledge of development and disabilities, to the partnership. The knowledge and strengths of both the family and professional are essential for creating and using effective strategies. The following stories identify both family and professional strengths that result in effective strategies the family can use.

> Danicka suggests that Mrs. Liang keep Jia close to her body when possible for bonding and attachment. Mrs. Liang said that she has her grandmother's wrap she used to carry her own children in, but Mrs. Liang is not sure how to wrap Jia with her medical needs. Danicka asks Mrs. Liang if the wrap is easy to find so they can figure out how best to use the wrap with Jia.

In this scenario, Danicka brings the specialized developmental knowledge and strategies of how this medically fragile infant could be best supported. Mrs. Liang builds on that knowledge by identifying a material, the wrap, which is already a part of her family and important for her to use as a family heirloom. The family–professional partnership then determines the best way to use the material to meet the child's developmental need.

> During a home visit, Mr. Johnson states that he has been reading books to his 26-month-old child, Manny. He does this because he knows how important it is to begin reading at an early age and it seems that Manny enjoys reading with his father. The early interventionist asks to watch Mr. Johnson and Manny when they read. During the observation, the early interventionist commends Mr. Johnson on the way he engages Manny in looking at and touching the pictures, and saying words for his son to hear and try to imitate. She then suggests that Mr. Johnson try propping up Manny so his back is straighter against the back of the couch. That might help Manny see better and more easily use his hands to touch the pictures.

In this scenario, Mr. Johnson brings to the partnership a routine activity that frequently occurs in his family's life that he knows his son enjoys—reading. He brings strategies he already uses to promote his child's development—naming pictures and engaging Manny to look at and touch pictures. The professional brings the ability to be an outside observer to see how the routine activity is currently helping Manny learn, and the ability to fine-tune the strategies Mr. Johnson is already using by changing Manny's positioning. This family–professional partnership optimizes Manny's development by creating strategies that are even more effective.

> At the end of the home visit, Ms. Epps says that she would like to begin taking Malika to the park to play. Her interventionist suggests that they go on the next intervention visit. They could use the slide, swings, riding apparatus, and sand box at the park. Ms. Epps

states that the park equipment sounded great, but she didn't think Malika would like the sand. She's noticed Malika doesn't like the feel of different textures, such as a certain rug in their home and the grass outside. The interventionist further discusses Ms. Epps's observations. Together, they decide this is something to look into further. When she leaves the Epps's home, the interventionist will ask the occupational therapist at the early intervention program to come to the park with them, since the occupational therapist has expertise in sensory issues.

In this scenario, the family brings an understanding of the child's unique characteristics, which in this case happens to be a developmental concern. In other situations, it may be a child's interest or temperament style. Because families know their child well, they can anticipate and predict the result of certain strategies suggested. The professional brings knowledge of the range of typical development—what's unique but not worrisome and when there might be a developmental concern that warrants another professional's advice. The professional also brings resources, such as the occupational therapist. Together, the family–professional partnership has the knowledge and resources to determine next steps in supporting Malika's development.

The Carminas and Patrice discuss ways to talk about Charlie's developmental needs to others. Patrice mentions a couple of ways that might help get them started, including talking to families who have already done this, or reviewing written materials and videos that talk about ways to begin the discussion. The Carminas agree that they are private people and are not ready to talk to other families. They would prefer to look at the videos and written materials.

In this scenario, the family brings knowledge of their own learning style and preferred strategies to meet their family outcomes. The professional has both written and audiovisual materials that can accommodate the family's preferences. Together, the family–professional partnership can use the resources that best fit the individual family to meet their priorities.

Each family brings knowledge and information about their own family, what's important to them, and what they want for their child. They bring cultural traditions and routines, materials, and objects. They know their child's nuances and what the family is already doing to support their child's development. The intervention professional provides knowledge of child development and children with disabilities, strategies to promote child development, and resources such as materials and other professionals. The knowledge and strengths of both family and professional are the foundation for effective, individualized supports.

Flexibility

Some families' lives are more predictable than others, but inevitably changes happen. These changes might be momentous, such as the birth of a child. These changes might be less meaningful, but no less significant, such as an unexpected insurance bill. Early intervention strives to fit seamlessly in each family's life, and therefore remains flexible and adjusts to the family's priorities. This includes being open to changes in the focus and schedule of intervention visits.

Intervention Focus. Together, the family–professional partnership identifies what to focus on during intervention visits. Certainly, the outcomes on the Individualized Family Service Plan (IFSP) would be one focus of the intervention. But which IFSP outcomes are addressed during each visit are decided on by the partnership. Does the family want to focus on a specific child or family outcome? This might be planned at a previous visit, but it might change by the next visit. Using the Johnson family above as an example, Mr. Johnson and the professional might have decided that at the next visit they would continue to focus on Manny "reading." However, when the interventionist arrives, Mr. Johnson's priority has changed. New priorities might arise because:

- The child has learned something new. Perhaps Mr. Johnson observed Manny's interest and emerging competence in concepts, such as colors, numbers, or size, while playing with toys. Mr. Johnson wants to promote these new competencies while Manny is ready and interested.
- A developmental concern has emerged. Perhaps Manny is having a hard time going from playtime to bedtime. Mr. Johnson might want to address this concern rather than the original plan for the visit.
- The family is focused on something going on in their family. For example, the professional might arrive to find Mr. Johnson on the phone with the insurance company, trying to remedy one of Manny's medical bills. Mr. Johnson might decide that this is more important at that moment. Mr. Johnson and the interventionist might decide to reschedule the visit. Or, the interventionist might stay and support Mr. Johnson figure out the medical bill.

The family–professional partnership might want to touch base in between visits to see if the plan for the intervention visit has changed. Even with a phone call, however, one never knows until the actual visit what might arise. Therefore, the focus of the visit might be tentatively planned ahead of time, but open to change at any time.

Schedule of Visits. The time when visits occur also requires flexibility. Intervention visits are scheduled during the times when routine activities actually occur (see next section). When intervention visits can vary in the times they occur, families are supported in using strategies during different routine activities. That way, the family can use the strategies throughout the child's day, and provide multiple opportunities for learning. For example, maybe certain strategies are working well during lunchtime when no one is home except the parent and child. During dinnertime, however, the family has not been able to figure out how to use the strategies when all six family members are home. Or, the family is happy using certain strategies while spending time outside, but not sure how the strategies can be used while cleaning up after dinner. Intervention visits can be scheduled at various times to partner during different routine activities. Flexibility in scheduling allows professionals to support families as they promote their child's development in a variety of routine activities.

There may also be times when the family finds it hard to focus on early intervention during the routine activity. For example, a family might have thought they would like to use intervention strategies during the morning when the family is getting ready to start their day. However, when it actually came time for the visit, the family found that the morning was too hectic to actually think about specific strategies.[4] The family and professional might decide to change the strategies to better fit the morning routine. Or, they might decide that the morning is going well, but it is not a good time to include specific strategies. Flexibility in scheduling allows intervention visits to fit into family life instead of family life being rearranged for interventions.

The keys to collaboration between families and professionals are a common purpose, family and professional strengths, and flexibility. When the family–professional partnership is successful, the family is comfortable and able to use strategies that promote their child's development in between intervention visits during the routine activities of everyday life.[5]

WHERE INTERVENTION VISITS OCCUR:
ROUTINE ACTIVITIES (AGAIN)

The importance of routine activities in child learning and development was explored in Chapter 2. As described, routine activities are the time when children learn and practice different developmental competencies in general, as well as the specific values and priorities of the individual family. Routine activities are when families help their children learn and develop. Families of young children with developmental delays or disabilities do not need to add extra activities to their day. What they need is guidance on how to make the most of the routine activities that are already occurring. Just like assessments (see Chapter 4), intervention visits occur in these *authentic* settings. That way, both the family and professional know that the learning strategies agreed upon actually work in the activities when the family will use them. Intervention visits are authentic when:

The visit occurs at the same day and time when the routine activity occurs.
Getting dressed will look very different if it occurs at 8 a.m., the usual
time the child needs to get dressed, versus 4 p.m. At 8 a.m., the child
might be tired, the parent stressed, or there might be other children who
also need help getting dressed and ready at that time. Therefore, instead
of scheduling intervention visits at any convenient time, the visit occurs
during the same time the routine activity usually occurs.

*Planned visits to focus on family outcomes are scheduled at a time that makes
sense for the family and does not interfere with other routine activities.*
The Carminas and Patrice work on ways to talk about Charlie's delays
after working on the bedtime routine with Charlie. That way, the
Carminas do not have to carve out time within their busy schedule to
meet with Patrice. While this works best for the Carminas and Patrice,
families might identify other down times when they can focus on family
outcomes, such as nap time, before other children come home from
school, or when the child is happy playing by him or herself.

*The people who usually comprise the routine activity participate in the routine
activity during the intervention visit.* When professionals come to visit,
families might feel that, to reduce distractions, family members, friends,
or others who are usually a part of the routine activity should leave. In
reality, these individuals will be a part of the routine activity when the
family uses the strategies in between intervention visits. Therefore, they
should be a part of the routine activity during the intervention visit.

*The toys, objects, and other materials used are already a part of the routine
activity.* In the first opening story of this chapter, the intervention
professional used materials she brought into the home. She also took
them with her when she was done. When professionals do this, the child
no longer has the same materials to practice with in between visits. The
family is left not only without the materials, but also without knowing
if the developmental strategies used during the visit will work with *their*
materials.

Any materials suggested or brought become the family's materials. Sometimes,
new materials are needed to promote development. For example, the
interventionist might bring a mat that keeps Manny from slipping on
the couch to help him sit. This material is given to Mr. Johnson so he can
continue to use the mat in between visits.

NATURAL LEARNING STRATEGIES

During intervention visits, the family and professional discuss and agree upon strategies the family will use during routine activities in between visits. Recommended

practices suggest that these strategies are *embedded* into the routine activities.[6] In other words, the strategies fit the routine activity rather than changing the routine activity to fit the strategies. To make sure they are using natural learning strategies, the family–professional partnership can discuss the following questions:

Do the strategies use the family's customs and traditions?[7]

Example (Child Outcome): Instead of the professional suggesting a commercially made baby carrier for Mrs. Liang, or one made especially for infants with complex medical needs, they used the wrap Mrs. Liang already had and valued.

Example (Family Outcome): In Chapter 3, the Carminas rely on family and friends for any child care needs they have, while Sean and Jolie prefer to use center-based child care and a professional babysitting service.

Does the strategy fit the family's values and ways of being?

Example (Child Outcome): There is a generally accepted strategy to promote communication by continually talking to the child about the child's actions. However, a particular family finds it uncomfortable to use this strategy because they do not talk very much in their everyday interactions. Instead, the strategy is changed to use the family's oral tradition of story telling at family gatherings. This strategy better fits this family.

Example (Family Outcome): The Carminas said they were private people and preferred written resources instead of speaking with other families.

Is the strategy doable or easy for the family?[8]

Example (Child Outcome): Instead of Mr. Johnson trying to balance the book, attend to Manny's positioning, and help him point, Mr. Johnson just has to put the mat on the couch and Manny can sit up when they are reading stories.

Example (Family Outcome): A parent finds it difficult to travel to night school after working all day, and to pay for babysitting in order to get her degree. Instead, the parent and professional found a program where most of the classes were online and could be completed at home.

Does the strategy fit with the way the routine activity occurs without dramatically changing it?

Example: The family wanted strategies to make transitioning between activities easier for their child to handle. Instead of taking the child to a picture chart hanging in the kitchen each time a different routine activity occurs, the family carries a small packet of pictures to show the child they are changing routine activities.

Does the strategy make the routine activity flow more smoothly or reduce stress?
Example: An initial strategy for quadruplets to learn to drink from a cup was to give them small amounts of liquid (to reduce spilling) in a cup without a lid. However, the parent is not able to keep up with each child to make sure they don't spill or run out of juice. Instead, the professional found cups with lids that have lips like an open cup. That way, the parent can fill each child's cup and not worry about spilling.

During intervention visits, it is very easy for a smooth working partnership to try out strategies together as a team. For example, the professional might hold the book while Mr. Johnson keeps Manny in a good position to use his hands. However, if the purpose of the visit is to support the family in using the strategies in between the intervention visits when the professional is not there, then the strategies need to be ones the family can do without the professional. If the strategy requires two people to implement, and usually there is only one adult available, then the strategy does not fit the family's routine activity. The overarching question to ask is, "If the interventionist is taken out of the routine activity, can the strategies suggested still occur?"[9]

The family–professional partnership creatively and collaboratively determines the best strategies so the child can participate and learn in routine activities. Bernheimer and Keogh summarized the importance of using strategies that fit the family's routine activities: "interventions fail . . . when they do not fit the daily routine of the family . . . when the intervention cannot be incorporated into the daily routine, or when the intervention is not compatible with the goals, values, and beliefs of the parents."[10] The most effective interventions fit the particular family and their ways of being, to promote child learning, engagement, and participation.

CHILD PARTICIPATION AND ENGAGEMENT STRATEGIES

During intervention visits, the family–professional partnership identifies and agrees on strategies that will promote the child learning the outcomes the family desires. Intervention strategies are based on what we know about child development discussed in Chapter 2. Specifically, intervention strategies:

- are tailored to the child's individual learning characteristics;
- build interest, participation, and engagement in the child's everyday routine activities; and
- provide just enough challenge for learning to occur.

Together, the family–professional partnership identifies strategies that best fit the child, the family's routine activities, *and* the family's individual culture.

Strategies that fit routine activities are functional and make sense in the specific routine activity.[11] For example, while playing with blocks, a nonfunctional strategy is asking the child to point to the red block. It doesn't make sense as part of play. However, a functional strategy is to ask the child to share a red block. The child is learning both sharing and colors. Strategies might be nonfunctional in an effort to create multiple opportunities to practice. But if the activity occurs over and over again without purpose, functionality is lost. This can be confusing to children as they try to understand why and when new competencies are used. Table 6.1 shows nonfunctional and functional ways to embed strategies.

Sometimes, it can be difficult to determine how the child can participate during specific therapeutic strategies. Some strategies might entail "doing to" the child, such as an adult stretching the child's muscles.[12] The family–professional partnership can identify ways to pair these kinds of strategies with ways the child can participate. For example, the child might "say" when she is ready for the next stretching exercise or choose which arm or leg to stretch next. This may require some creativity from the family–professional partnership, but it adheres to the principles of how young children learn and develop.[13] Children learn by actively participating, and by the partnership considering, all aspects of a child's development, such as choice making (for example, choosing which arm or leg), initiative (for example, deciding when to start), and communication (for example, saying when to start), rather than isolating one component, such as his or her muscles.

The intervention visit is the time to determine if strategies work while the professional is there to help figure out how best to use the strategies.[14] For example, if Jia cries while in the wrap, the family–professional partnership looks for reasons why the baby is unhappy and ways to fix the situation. When successful strategies are found during the intervention visit, families are armed with strategies they know work before they are expected to use them on their own in between visits.

Table 6.1. Nonfunctional and Functional Ways for Practice Opportunities

Nonfunctional	*Functional*
Child walks up stairs and then is brought down to climb again	Child climbs the stairs of the slide and slides down, then climbs the stairs to slide again
Child waves goodbye to someone who then comes back in the room for the child to wave goodbye again	Child waves goodbye to each individual as his parents and two siblings leave for the day
Child climbs into the car seat only to be taken out of the car to climb in again	Child climbs in and out of the car seat during errands, making frequent stops

FAMILY COMPETENCE AND ABILITY WITH CHILD OUTCOMES

Let's look back at the two examples at the beginning of this chapter. While the parent in the first example is participating in the home visit—watching and listening to the professional, and motivating, praising, and soothing the child—the parent is not learning how to use the strategies. In this example, the focus is on the child learning during the intervention visit. In the second example, the parent is discussing, observing, and trying out strategies. In this example, the focus is on the parent learning the strategies so they can be used to help the child learn during the multiple opportunities that occur in between intervention visits. By the end of this intervention visit, the family will feel comfortable with, and be able to use, the strategies to effectively promote their child's development.

Many studies in early intervention have found that families can and do learn to use strategies that promote their child's development.[15] But, just like any adult learning something new, families need the opportunity to understand and practice with professional support. Consider any skill you enjoy watching—dancing, sports, cooking, or any of the skills on some reality television shows. Even though you watch a person "doing" the skill, can you then competently do that skill yourself? Unless you are someone who already has some background in it, most likely the answer is "no." Therefore, in early intervention, it is not enough for families to sit back and watch while the professional uses strategies with the child. Now consider some of the cooking and home improvement shows that walk through how they actually complete their meals or projects. These shows provide more information about how to do that skill. But what if, when you try to do it, your attempt doesn't look like the experts' on the show? What if the results are not the same? How will you figure out what's going on? The same concept applies in early intervention. Families can watch professionals as they demonstrate and explain how to use a strategy, but that just isn't enough. What if the family runs into snags, like what happened with the recipe or the project? Families and professionals need to know that the strategies work before families are left to use the strategies on their own.[16] So now, let's think about when these shows have guests who are learning from the experts. The experts explain what they're going to do and why. They might show the guest how to do certain parts, but they actually let the guest complete the recipe or project, with the experts there to support as needed. That way, the guests know they can do it on their own. In other words, the experts coach the guests so the guests learn. Early intervention uses this same method to make sure that families feel comfortable and competent in using the strategies that will promote their child's development. In order to do this, the family–professional partnership will:

- agree on a strategy;
- model or demonstrate;
- practice or try out; and
- provide feedback.

Let's look at each one of these components.

Agree on a Strategy

Family members and professionals collaborate to decide on a strategy to try. Part of this conversation is identifying *why* a strategy might work. When a professional or a family member identifies a potential strategy, the questions to be discussed are:

- How will the strategy help this particular child learn?
- Why might this strategy work for this particular child?

As clearly stated in the questions, the answers should make sense based on the child's unique learning characteristics and the family's unique priorities. Some might assume that the professional provides the rationale for a strategy. In fact, professionals are responsible for explaining the research and effectiveness behind potential strategies, but the rationale is really built as a partnership. Below is an example of how the family–professional partnership built a rationale for using the wrap with Jia Liang:

- Mrs. Liang explained to Danicka that she wanted to promote Jia's strength in regulation by reducing the amount of time she holds Jia. However, whenever she puts her down, Jia becomes very disorganized.
- Danicka agreed that Jia could learn to self-regulate when things aren't too overly stimulating to her. However, Jia does seem to use her mother's holding as a way to regulate. Danicka added that she knew bonding with Jia was an important priority for Mrs. Liang, which holding helped with, especially when Jia needed outside regulation.
- Mrs. Liang affirmed that bonding was still very important to her, but that it was getting harder and harder for her to hold Jia all the time.
- Danicka thought that a wrap could be used instead. That way, the baby would be snuggled against Mrs. Liang, but Mrs. Liang would also have her hands free to do other things.
- Mrs. Liang asked if Danicka thought it would work, even though she wouldn't be physically holding Jia.
- Danicka thought it could work as an in-between step because Jia would be physically against her mother, and if she needed to be held, Mrs. Liang was right there to provide more support. She thought Jia was ready for this step and asked if Mrs. Liang was ready for it too.

In this example, the family and professional each contributed to building a case for why the wrap might work. When a strategy is agreed on, both the family and professional should be able to explain why the strategy might work. The professional can ask questions to make sure this is the case. The family can ask questions if they do not know why they are using a certain strategy, or how the strategy will help their child meet certain outcomes. For example, Mr. Johnson might ask the early interventionist, "We want Manny to learn to sit by himself. Won't using this mat make it easier for him to sit? How will he learn to sit without it?" The early interventionist might explain that the mat will make it easier for Manny to sit. But Manny is actually using his abdominal muscles more than when he's slouched over. So the strategy helps Manny in storybook reading, as well as builds his physical development for sitting. The family–professional partnership comes to a common understanding of why a strategy might be tried.

Model or Demonstrate

For some strategies, the professional might demonstrate to the family how to use a certain strategy. The purpose of modeling is so the family can see what the strategy looks like. Modeling is *not* the professional working with the child while the family watches, or participates as the family did in the first example at the beginning of the chapter. While the professional demonstrates, the family and professional are talking about:

- what the professional is doing (for example, the steps to the strategy); and
- how the child responded to the strategy (for example, how does the child look different when the strategy is used versus when it wasn't used).

In modeling, the family is actively participating by watching and talking about the strategy so the family is prepared to try the strategy themselves.

Practice or Try It Out

The only true way to know if a strategy works for a particular child and a particular family is for the family to try out the strategy during the intervention visit, when the interventionist is there.[17] That way, the family–professional partnership can see how well the strategy works for the family and, if necessary, fine-tune the strategy or find another strategy, to fit the family. While the family is trying out the strategy, the early intervention professional is encouraging, guiding, and answering questions. For example, while Mr. Johnson is sitting Manny on the mat, the interventionist might suggest that he scoot Manny's hips further back, or point out how less stiff Manny's arms look. While there may be times when the early intervention professional might help the family learn a strategy, by the end of the visit the family should be able to successfully use the strategy without the interventionist.[18] This is important because the interventionist won't be there to help the family during the routine activities in between the visits. If the strategy cannot be done without the interventionist helping, then a new strategy is identified. For example, if Danicka keeps helping Mrs. Liang put on the wrap and position Jia in the wrap, what will Mrs. Liang do when Danicka is not there to help? Trying out the strategies while the interventionist is there shows both the family and the interventionist that the family can easily use the strategy in between intervention visits.

Provide Feedback

Throughout the intervention visit, open and honest communication is critical. The family–professional partnership is continually discussing the strategies and whether the strategies work for the child and the family. The following are potential questions to discuss:

- Was the strategy effective? Did it have the desired effect on the child's learning and participation?
- How did the strategy feel for the family? Is the family comfortable with it?
- Does the family feel the strategy can be used in everyday life? Is the strategy doable given the family's schedule and lifestyle, and how they interact?

By having this conversation, the family–professional partnership can identify the best strategies for the family to use during their routine activities, in between intervention visits.

The four components described above are frequently used to help families feel confident and competent in using the agreed upon strategies. However, the family–professional partnership ultimately decides the best way to support the family. This will depend on the type of strategy and the family's individual characteristics:

Some strategies may only need to be discussed. For example, the mother of the quadruplets will simply obtain and use the specific type of sippy cup for the children to drink from. Nothing really needs to be modeled or tried out in the presence of the interventionist. That said, the interventionist checks in with the mother to make sure that the sippy cup is working for the family.

Modeling is dependent on both the strategy and the family characteristics. For example, Mr. Johnson does not need the interventionist to model how to use the mat. But unlike the sippy cup example, this family–professional partnership does try out the strategy while the interventionist is there to help make sure that the mat serves its purpose for Manny.

As another example, Mrs. Liang might know how to use the wrap because she used it with her other children. She doesn't need Danicka to show her (or model) how to use the wrap. What she needs to know is how to use the wrap for her youngest baby in particular. In this situation, because of what Mrs. Liang already knows how to do, the family–professional partnership might skip modeling and Mrs. Liang would try out the strategy with Danicka there for support. Modeling may also be skipped if a family member feels like s/he learns best by doing, and wants to try out a strategy instead of watching it first. Then, if needed, they might want the interventionist to model.

While the components for supporting family strategy use are determined by the family–professional partnership, any time modeling is used calls for the family to try out the strategies. That way, the family and the professional know that the family is able, and feels comfortable, using those strategies.

FAMILY COMPETENCE AND ABILITY WITH FAMILY OUTCOMES

These same steps can be applied to family outcomes. Below, the components are illustrated when working on the Carminas' outcome of talking to others about Charlie's developmental needs:

> *Agree on a strategy.* Patrice asked the Carminas to identify the strategies in the written materials they think are good ones to try. Both Elizabeth and Joseph agreed that writing down a couple of sentences they can have on hand would be helpful. They *explained* that, when the time comes, they won't have to think on their feet. Patrice supported their thoughts by *clarifying* that it sounded like sometimes they're taken aback by what someone says or does and can't think of the words. The parents agreed.
> *Model or demonstrate.* The Carminas had some trouble coming up with the right words. Patrice eased their concerns by saying that this is exactly why they're practicing. She said that the words definitely had to be theirs, but she provided some *examples* of general sentences the family could start with. They could tailor them to specifically what they wanted to say.
> *Practice or try it out.* The Carminas began to *come up* with some sentences and phrases they wanted to use. They *tried them out on each other, role playing* the different people they came across in the past.
> *Provide feedback.* Patrice asked the Carminas *how they felt* about the sentences they came up with. Elizabeth said she *wanted to change* a few words, but was happy with it and it was *easier than she had thought.* Joseph said he could feel himself getting angry and *it might be hard for him* to remember the words in the moment, but knows getting angry is not the answer. Patrice said that, while Joseph may have been feeling angry, *she thought* he did not come across angry. Patrice and Joseph began to think of ways for him to relax so he can recall what he wants to say.

ARE INTERVENTIONS WORKING?

Clearly, the goals of early intervention are for each child to learn, develop, and meet the outcomes and vision of the family. But as discussed throughout this book, children are learning all the time as they participate in their typical family life. Therefore, the more accurate goal of early intervention is for the child to develop *more* (that is, at a faster rate, improved quality of competencies, and so forth) than he or she would have without early intervention. Specific questions to ask are:

- Are the strategies working?
- Are the strategies helping the child learn and develop?

To answer these questions, the family–professional partnership must look at the two expected outcomes of intervention visits—the child's participation and learning in everyday routine activities and the family's use of agreed upon intervention strategies in everyday routine activities.

As discussed in Chapter 2, children have mastered new competencies when they can easily use the competency anywhere, anytime. To know if the child has, or is beginning to, master the intervention outcomes, the family–professional partnership asks:

- What is new or different about the way the child is participating in routine activities? What is the child doing differently?
- Have there been glimpses of the competency emerging? Has the child exhibited the competency?
- Where has the child shown the competency or its emergence? How often has the child shown the competency or its emergence?

These questions allow the family–professional partnership to identify whether the child is making progress toward, or has mastered, the expected competencies.

Even if child progress is seen, it doesn't necessarily mean that early intervention or the strategies agreed on had a role in the child's progress. Families use many strategies to help their child learn—some from early intervention, some they figure out themselves.[19] It is important to know whether the intervention strategies work, because that information helps the family–professional partnership understand how the child learns. This information can be used to create new strategies so the child can learn new, more sophisticated, competencies. To understand this, the family–professional partnership asks:

When were the strategies used in between visits? Strategies need to be used multiple times in multiple activities for children to learn and generalize. If the strategies were not used in a variety of places, the strategies were less likely to have contributed to child progress. If strategies are not used, the family–professional partnership can discuss why, and determine whether to try the strategies again, modify them, or come up with completely new strategies.

Were the strategies used the way they were used in the visit? Some changes might make the strategy fit better in the family's routine activity, and therefore increase the strategy's effectiveness. But some changes might decrease the strategy's effectiveness.[20] If the strategy was changed, and the child did not show the expected progress, it might not mean the strategy doesn't work. It may just mean that it didn't work the way it was used. The family–professional partnership can use this information to determine whether to try the strategies again, modify them, or come up with completely new strategies.

During the intervention visit, the more the family and professional collaborate to create intervention strategies that fit the family, the more likely the strategies will be used in the routine activities so the child can learn. It is up to the family–professional partnership—during the intervention visit—to clearly describe the strategy, identify the parts or steps of the strategy that are important for the strategy to be effective, and how the strategy can be changed.[21]

Even if a strategy is clearly discussed and practiced during the intervention visit, a family might feel less comfortable with the strategy once they use it as part of everyday life. For example, at first, a family might have felt comfortable waiting for a child to say part of a word before giving him what he requested by pointing. But as the family used it during their routine activities, the family began to feel less comfortable. They thought that the child was getting too upset. They also felt that they were ignoring the child's communication of pointing, and that the child would stop pointing because it wasn't working. They thought that would result in the child feeling like he was not understood by his family. The family–professional partnership openly discusses and respects these concerns. Then, they find ways to meet the family's goals according to their beliefs.

The family–professional partnership determines the best way to keep track of child progress and the strategy use that occurs in between visits. Some families keep a checklist handy, like on the refrigerator door. Other families write in a journal at the end of the day. Sometimes, the interventionist will call to check in and ask about the strategies used. Other times, progress and strategies are discussed and observed at the next intervention visit. Whatever method is chosen by the family–professional partnership, it should be easy for the family and provide accurate information on whether the intervention is working.

THE BIG PICTURE: RELATED POLICIES AND GUIDELINES

The federal legislation does not discuss actual intervention visits that much. The guidance for the visit comes during the IFSP meeting, when interventions are planned (see Chapter 5). Also, recommended practices are more focused on the specific types of strategies used during intervention visits. There are, however, relevant recommended practices. The Division for Early Childhood of the Council for Exceptional Children (DEC) expressly recommends that intervention "team members focus on the between-sessions times" as the times when child learning truly occurs.[22] Recommended practices further specify that early intervention should focus on child engagement and learning within routine activities, and use strategies that are individualized, attuned to the characteristics of the routine activities, and known to be effective. For all outcomes, the family–professional partnership is essential and interventions are tailored to the characteristics of the family, including their priorities, culture, and beliefs. While these guidelines are broad, there is literature that provides practical guidance on how intervention visits should occur.

SUMMARY:
A PARTNERSHIP LEARNING TOGETHER

Early intervention visits are the time when the family–professional partnership collaborates to meet child and family outcomes. By the end of the visit, the family–professional partnership should know that the family can use, and feel comfortable using, the strategies agreed upon to promote child learning and address their family priorities. Only through a back and forth sharing of each other's thoughts, ideas, and questions can this be achieved.

Preparing for the Partnership: What Families Bring

The following questions can be considered by family members as they prepare for participation in intervention visits:

Family–Professional Collaboration

What questions do you have about how intervention visits will occur or your role in the visits?

Who else in your family or social network needs to know about how early intervention works?

What are you already doing to help your child learn? How would you describe your strengths in helping him or her learn?

Natural Learning Environments and Strategies

When should intervention visits occur? When do the targeted routine activities occur? What are good times to address family outcomes?

Who usually participates in the routine activities? Do they know about early intervention?

Family Confidence and Ability

What questions do you have about why you are learning to use intervention strategies?

What questions do you have about why certain strategies are recommended? Why do you think the strategies are being used?

How would you describe your learning style?

What kinds of strategies are important for you to see demonstrated? What kinds of strategies need to be tried out versus only discussed?

What questions do you have about providing feedback on strategies? How comfortable do you feel doing this? What do you need in order to feel comfortable?

What is the best way for you to keep track of your child's progress and intervention strategies in between visits?

Preparing for the Partnership: What Professionals Bring

The following questions can be considered by early intervention professionals as they prepare for participation in intervention visits:

Family–Professional Collaboration

How will you explain how intervention visits occur? What information do you need to explain this?

Who are the other team members who need to know about early intervention?

How will you find out about the family's strengths and what they are already doing to help their child learn?

Natural Learning Environments and Strategies

How will you find out when intervention visits should occur? How will you find out when targeted routine activities occur?

How will you make sure that the routine activity occurs as it usually does in everyday life?

How will you tailor strategies to fit the values and characteristics of this family?

Family Confidence and Ability

How will you explain why your role is to support families so that they can use intervention strategies in between visits?

How will you collaborate with the family in building a reason for specific strategies? How will you describe the rationale and evidence base behind the strategies being used?

How will you uncover the family's learning style?

How will you know that you are modeling strategies versus working directly with the child?

What strategies do you want to see tried out versus only discussed?

How comfortable do you feel providing feedback to families about strategies tried? How comfortable do you feel about eliciting feedback from families about strategies tried? What do you need in order to feel comfortable?

What methods of data collection can you offer as examples for families to document progress and strategy use in between visits?

Chapter 7

JOINING THE COMMUNITY

Each morning, Fatima walks her 8-year-old child, Antwon, to the bus stop, while pushing 23-month-old Ciera in her stroller. After the bus picks up Antwon, Fatima and Ciera walk three blocks to the construction site in their neighborhood. They watch the construction crew and the different construction equipment, which Ciera just loves. They then walk another block to their local library. There, Fatima picks out books for herself, finds the books Antwon has requested, and looks for any new books for Ciera. Then, they walk back home.

Each morning, Jolie Simmons drops off her twins, Aiden and Elliot, at the child care center in the basement of Jolie's corporation. There, the boys watch other children and are beginning to interact with them. They have a lot of time to play. There's singing, materials to explore, and space to move around. The teachers make sure that all of the boys' care needs are met, and that Elliot gets his medication on time. Since Jolie has long hours, Sean picks the boys up after work. While things are hectic in the classroom, as many families are picking up their children, Sean makes sure he has a couple of minutes with the teacher to find out about Aiden and Elliot's day.

Children grow up in families, and families live in communities. Communities are suburban neighborhoods, city blocks, and rural towns. Few would disagree. But what many might not think about is that, as with the routine activities that occur in the home, communities are full of routine activities where learning occurs. In other words, places like grandparent's house, neighborhood playgrounds, child care, and even the grocery store, are where families live and children learn.

ROUTINE ACTIVITIES IN THE COMMUNITY

Just like the routine activities that occur in the home, community routine activities are simply *what families and children do* as part of their everyday lives. And just like routine activities in the home, community routine activities are full of learning opportunities for young children.[1] In the first story above, Ciera is walking to the bus stop and around her community, watching construction, and visiting the library. Some potential learning opportunities for Ciera are:

- to go out in her stroller and do things;
- to say goodbye to her brother;
- words associated with construction like *crane, up, down,* and *dumptruck*; and
- how to work with books, such as turning pages and holding the book right side up.

In the second story, while in child care, Aiden and Elliot are singing, playing and exploring, and getting their needs met. They are learning to:

- interact with others;
- understand the properties of different objects; and
- communicate their needs.

These are just a few possible competencies each child can learn. Intervention strategies that are based on each child's unique learning characteristics are embedded into these community activities. This provides more enhanced opportunities for the child to learn and master emerging skills and competencies.[2]

KINDS OF COMMUNITY ACTIVITIES

There are many different community activities families may do in everyday life.[3] Community activities may be:

Formal: Activities that are purposely designed to be learning opportunities. These activities are those occurring in child care and any parent–child classes, including swimming, baby sign language, music, and baby exercise classes.

Casual: Activities available to families but not structured as learning opportunities, such as parks, libraries, and playgrounds.

Practical: Activities that are part of a family's routines to get their family priorities met. Examples include going to the grocery store, waiting for the bus, or walking the dog. These may not be thought of as specific learning opportunities, but they do provide various experiences to participate and learn.

Impromptu: Activities families might not have thought of, but that came about because the experience happened to be available. Examples include stumbling upon a neighborhood fair, or going somewhere because the child showed great interest, such as a construction site.

Some early intervention programs create a "community map" of the types of activities that are available to families in their particular community.[4] While the map would most likely not include all the possible learning opportunities, especially all the practical and impromptu activities, it is a way for families to see the many possibilities available. Just like routine activities at home, the kinds of community routine activities each family participates in, and the expected competencies each child learns, is identified by the family and dependent on the family's values and priorities for their child's development.

Community routine activities can occur within a family's immediate neighborhood, such as on their block; or they might be a car, bus, or train ride away. Community activities also vary in terms of who participates. Community activities may be *family outings*, where the child participates with other family members. Family outings may not include community members, such as using self-check out at the grocery store. Or, family outings can include a community member, such as a librarian during "Babies 'n Books" hour or a swim coach during swimming classes. There may also be family activities when the child participates with other family members, and chance meetings occur with community members. Fatima and Ciera going for a walk and watching the construction site is one such example. The activity is really between the two of them, but construction workers or passersby may stop and talk to Fatima or Ciera. This also frequently occurs when going shopping and check out clerks or salespeople interact with the child and family. Community activities may also be *child experiences*, where the child participates with community members and not the family, such as child care or play dates. In these situations however, the family is still the provider of these opportunities and makes sure quality learning and care are occurring, as Sean did at Aiden and Elliot's child care by speaking with their teacher.

A COMMUNITY FOR ALL CHILDREN

Community routine activities are made up of learning opportunities for young children with and without developmental delays or disabilities. When children actively participate in these community activities, child development is promoted.[5] This may happen with or without the support of early intervention. However, early intervention can play a role in strengthening the ability of family and community members to make the most of these community activities as learning opportunities. A conversation among the family–professional partnership members can identify community routine activities where early intervention supports could be helpful. This conversation could center on community routine activities that:

- the child enjoys and participates in with his or her family (for example, Ciera going for walks to watch the construction);

- the child has a hard time participating in with his or her family, but has to participate (for example, a child who has a hard time at the grocery store, but the family has to go shopping);
- the child does not yet participate in but the family would like to do (such as hiking in the mountains as the family did before the child was born);[6]
- the child enjoys and participates in without the family (such as Aiden and Elliot participating in child care activities);
- the child has a hard time participating in without the family (for example, a child has a hard time transitioning in between activities that occur during child care); and
- the child does not yet participate in but the family would like the child to do without the family (for example, have the child join the drop-off care at the local gym so the parents can workout).[7]

Once the family–professional partnership identifies specific routine activities in the community where early intervention can occur, specific interventions can be planned and implemented. There has not been a lot of research done around community routine activities, especially outside child care.[8] However, it is assumed that the same processes used in home-based interventions can be used in community interventions. The family–professional partnership assesses how the child learns and participates in the particular routine activity and plans interventions there. Then, intervention visits occur using the concepts discussed in Chapter 6. The family–professional partnership decides if the strategies are effective in helping the child learn and develop, and whether the family feels confident and competent in using the strategies. There are some differences, however. These differences are described below for both community routine activities where family members participate and those where the child participates without the family.

Family Outings

Interventions can occur during community routine activities that both the family and child participate in. For example, the early intervention professional can collaborate with Fatima during their morning trip to the bus stop, construction site, and library. There are considerations specific to community intervention visits.

Explaining the Interventionist. Sometimes, community members might ask who the person is accompanying the family, especially if community members are used to seeing and interacting with the family in the routine activity. Sometimes, families have no problem explaining, or having the interventionist explain, that the early interventionist is helping with the child's development. Other times, families might want to keep early intervention confidential, and simply say the interventionist is a friend. The family–professional partnership can discuss ahead of time and determine the best way to address any questions.[9]

Coaching in the Community. The family–professional partnership might amend how the coaching relationship occurs when out in the community. For example, when checking out at the library, Ciera might look at the librarian and say, "Buh!" The interventionist might say to the librarian, "She wants to hold her book!" The librarian smiles at Ciera and gives her the book. When walking back home, the interventionist then discusses with Fatima how she helped the librarian understand Ciera's communication and whether Fatima might want to do that too. It might feel uncomfortable for Fatima and the librarian to have this conversation at the moment the interventionist modeled the strategy. It might also violate confidentiality. But the conversation still occurred, just later, between only Fatima and the interventionist.

Also in this situation, the interventionist is helping community members understand and interact with Ciera in her unique way, which might help them interact with other children of diverse abilities in the future. Fatima can also promote this when she uses strategies that help others interact with Ciera.

Identifying Community Appropriate Strategies. There may be some strategies that families feel comfortable using at home, but do not feel comfortable using in public. They may feel that the strategies stigmatize their child and therefore do not promote membership in the community.[10] Following the criteria discussed in Chapter 6 around embedding strategies will help ensure the strategies make sense. However, the family–professional partnership can also discuss whether the family feels comfortable using the strategies in public.

Child Experiences

Interventions can occur during community routine activities that the child participates in without the family. The considerations for family outings also hold true for these experiences. The family–professional partnership decides how to 1.) explain the intervention to others, such as other families participating in the activities, 2.) coach in the community, and 3.) identify community appropriate strategies to focus on membership and avoid stigma. There are additional considerations, however, that primarily center on including the community members responsible for the child in the early intervention process. These considerations are discussed below, using the example of community routine activities at Aiden and Elliot's child care center.

Including Community Members in Intervention Planning. If community members are expected to work with early intervention professionals during community routine activities, these community members need to be a part of the planning process.[11] This may also be true for family outings when a community member is leading an activity, such as "Babies 'n Books" or swimming classes. This planning includes making sure community members understand how early intervention works. For example, during the intervention meeting, Sean Crause explained to the boys' child care teacher how early intervention is there to support the teacher, but not take over, or take the boys out of the regular child care routine.

In addition, community members can be a part of planning by identifying routine activities where interventions can occur. In some situations, there is only one routine activity, such as the playing that occurs during drop-off child care at a family's gym. Other times, like full-day child care, there are a lot of routine activities that occur throughout the day. For example, during the Individualized Family Service Plan (IFSP) meeting, Aiden and Elliot's child care teacher talks about the learning opportunities she sees at child care, especially during those times of the day the boys are very interested in. She also would like support with diaper changing to make it go more smoothly for Aiden. Together, the family, early interventionist, and child care teacher identify the best routine activities to focus on— those activities the child is interested in and those that are challenging.

Ensuring Strategies Work for All in the Activity. As with strategies at home that need to fit the family's culture and how the routine activity occurs, strategies need to fit the philosophy of the program and the way the community activity occurs.[12] For example, in the child care center, strategies need to work for a class where teachers are responsible for the learning and care needs of many children in the class, not just Aiden and Elliot. The teachers need to feel comfortable with the strategies and feel the strategies fit with the *emergent curriculum* used, where the staff interact with and respond to the infants, attuned to the family's culture and values. While the early interventionist visits during the hectic routine activities of child care, she also comes during nap time to talk with the boy's child care teacher. That way, the discussion does not disrupt the daily activities of the child care day.

Coordinating with the Family. By definition, the family is not a regular part of these kinds of community routine activities. However, the family needs to be kept up-to-date on what early intervention is doing in these routine activities and how the family's priorities for child learning are being addressed. The family–professional partnership decides on the best way to do this. For example, on every visit, the early interventionist writes a summary of the visit. Aiden and Elliot's child care teacher copies the summary so both she and the family can have the summary as a reference. Also, during home intervention visits, the family–professional partners discuss what's happening at child care. As part of the conversation between the teacher and Sean, the teacher describes how the specific intervention strategies were used during the day. There have been times when Jolie was able to come from her office to watch what happens when the interventionist is present.

Early intervention supports can be provided in community settings. In many ways, these supports work the same as supports in the home. The family–professional partnership also considers the public nature of being out in the community, however, and the needs of all community members.

THE BIG PICTURE: RELATED POLICIES AND GUIDELINES

The early intervention legislation and recommended practices described in Chapter 6 hold true for early intervention in community routine activities. The focus on *membership* becomes more noteworthy in the community. Early intervention can help children with developmental delays and disabilities belong as accepted members of the community. A recommended practice specific to group community settings is related to the quality of care settings. The Division for Early Childhood of the Council for Exceptional Children (DEC) states that "learning environments [must] meet accepted standards of quality, including curriculum, child-staff ratios, group size, and physical design of the classroom."[13] In other words, early intervention professionals are responsible for supporting families to ensure that the community routine activities their child participates in are high quality for all children, with and without developmental delays or disabilities.

SUMMARY: JOINING THE COMMUNITY

Community routine activities are those everyday errands and play experiences, and special occasions that occur as part of a family's life within a community. Each family defines community, and the activities in it, for themselves. The family–professional partnership can take advantage of the learning opportunities available in these community routine activities. In so doing, they promote child learning and participation as a community member. They also help the community promote the particular child's learning and development, and be more prepared to promote the development of other children with diverse abilities.

Preparing for the Partnership: What Families Bring

The following questions can be considered by family members as they prepare for participation in community intervention visits (note that the questions in Chapter 6 should also be used when preparing for community interventions):

Community Activities

What kinds of experiences does your family or your child have outside the home? What are other kinds of experiences you would like for your family or your child?

What community routine activities would you like intervention to support? What would you like your child to learn during those routine activities?

Planning Community Interventions

How do you want to address questions about the interventionist when in the community?
Which community members could participate in intervention planning?
What questions do you have about coaching in the community?
What are important qualities of strategies used in the community to promote membership?
How do you want to participate in interventions that occur in community settings in which your child participates, but you do not? What are the best ways for you to stay informed?

Preparing for the Partnership: What Professionals Bring

The following questions can be considered by early intervention professionals as they prepare for participation in community intervention visits (note that the questions in Chapter 6 should also be used when preparing for community interventions):

Community Activities

How much do you know about the variety of learning opportunities available in the community?
Does your agency have a community map of the area?

Planning Community Interventions

How will you prepare with the family for questions from community members about who you are?
How will you discuss with the family coaching in the community? What do you need in order to effectively coach in the community?
What resources will you use to ensure strategies are community appropriate and promote membership?
What do you need in order to prepare to work with community members such as child care providers?
How will you describe how early intervention works?
How will you involve them in intervention planning and visits?
How will you collaborate with the family when interventions occur in child community experiences without the family?

Chapter 8

MAKING IT ALL MAKE SENSE

Let's look at the formal supports of two families from earlier chapters:

The Carmina family has two early intervention professionals on their team. Patrice, a physical therapist, is the Carminas' primary provider. She supports the family in promoting Charlie's learning and development. She also helps them figure out how to speak to others about Charlie's developmental needs, and to meet their family's priority around child care (now that both Joseph and Elizabeth are working). Jessica, a developmental specialist, is also a member of the Carminas' family–professional partnership. Jessica works with Patrice outside of intervention visits, and is available to come with her to intervention visits. Also, Charlie regularly sees his primary care pediatrician for medical checkups.

The family–professional partnership for the Coles-Williams family has a lot of team members. In addition to Dionne's parents and grandmother, there are the special instructor, Sarah, the occupational therapist, Julio, and the vision specialist, Regina. Sarah comes to the family's home 3 times a week. Julio comes with Sarah on two of those visits. Regina comes once a month with Sarah. Holly, the service coordinator, visits at least twice a month, and calls frequently as she partners with Kenisha and Gary to find quality child care for Dionne. Holly has also been in touch with the assistive technology (AT) program to schedule an evaluation at a good time for Dionne, Kenisha, Gary, and Julio. In addition to the early intervention partnership members, there are many medical professionals—Dionne's primary care pediatrician, a neurologist, an ophthalmologist for her vision, and a feeding team at the local children's hospital. The Coles-Williams family is applying to the Children with Special Health Care Needs program. They also receive equipment from a medical supplier. The family participates in a parent-to-parent program, where they are connected with a "veteran" family whose child has similar disabilities. Everyone is very valuable to the

Coles-Williams family. Still, there are a lot of people, information, and suggestions to think about.

Early intervention is a unique program that many are unfamiliar with. There are many aspects to early intervention and it can be difficult for families to know all the procedures and what should be expected. Families have to keep track of everything that's happening, make sense of the information they are getting, and stay on top of the supports provided. Most families are new to early intervention and have no more than 3 years to figure it out before they are no longer eligible. Most families could use support from someone who is an expert in how early intervention works, to help oversee and coordinate the family's early intervention experience. Early intervention offers support to organize the processes, programs, and professionals involved with families of infants and toddlers with developmental delays or disabilities. This support is called *service coordination*.

PULLING IT ALL TOGETHER

One day, Holly, the service coordinator, was leaving the Coles-Williamses' home at the same time that Gary's mother was arriving. After Holly left, Gary's mother said that she knew what the other early intervention professionals did, and met Holly at the meeting to create the Individualized Family Service Plan (IFSP), but didn't know what Holly actually did. Kenisha said, "Oh, Holly does lots of things. She's sort of the organizer—making sure that early intervention happens the way it's supposed to, and that all the professionals are on the same page. She knows a lot of people and programs, so she can tell us which local child care providers have experience with children who have similar needs as Dionne. She also knows how to get things done, like contacting the AT program to set up the evaluation and helping us enroll in the Children with Special Health Care Needs program. We could do it all ourselves, but Holly knows the 'ins and outs' of all these programs and does this for a lot of families. So it's less of a hassle for us. Oh, and Holly even makes sure that all the doctors know what's happening in early intervention and that early intervention knows what's happening with Dionne medically. This is so helpful, especially when Dionne is in the hospital."

Kenisha Coles clearly described the role of the service coordinator as the early intervention organizer. With the various team members and supports available to families of children with developmental delays or disabilities, families might appreciate someone who helps keep track of everything and connects with early intervention and other supports. Someone who understands early intervention, and can make sure that the professionals—inside and outside of early intervention—collaborate with one another. A coordinated effort is necessary so families can make sense of early intervention and that supports are helpful rather than disjointed and, possibly, overwhelming. In other words, the service coordinator makes sure that supports fit together to best meet the priorities of the individual family and child. That way, families and children aren't pulled in separate directions. Instead, supports are pulled together.

Early Intervention Service Coordination

Each family–professional partnership has a service coordinator who is the team facilitator. However, all team members are responsible for ensuring that supports are coordinated. What needs to be coordinated in early intervention?

Early Intervention Processes. Both the Carminas and Coles-Williamses went through the processes of getting into early intervention and planning interventions. They are both currently participating in intervention visits and regularly scheduled reviews of the intervention plan.

Early Intervention Programs. Early intervention professionals can come from one agency or program, like Patrice and Jessica of the Carmina family–professional partnership. Or, they can come from different agencies or programs. The Coles-Williams family–professional partnership is comprised of three programs. Regina, the vision specialist, is from a different program than Holly, Sarah, and Julio. The AT specialists responsible for the assistive technology evaluation are at yet another program.

The Family–Professional Partnership. Each family–professional partnership is comprised of different team members. The Carminas have two early intervention professionals and the Coles-Williamses have three regular early intervention professionals, plus those involved with the AT evaluation. Team members are coordinated so families do not have too many (or too few) visits and recommendations do not contradict one another (see Chapter 5). That way, as Kenisha Coles said, everyone is "on the same page."

Table 8.1 lists potential questions the family–professional partnership might ask as they coordinate early intervention processes, programs, and professionals.

Specific Service Coordination Tasks

As Kenisha Coles described, there are many tasks of service coordination. These include:

Table 8.1. Sample Questions Service Coordination Addresses

Areas	Questions
Processes	What does a family do to enroll in early intervention? What is required for eligibility?
	How does a family who was in early intervention in another community enroll in early intervention in a new community?
	Who will organize the creation and review of intervention plans?
	Who does the family go to if intervention visits don't fit the family?
	How are different components of early intervention paid for?
	How does the family–professional partnership prepare the family to leave early intervention when they're no longer eligible? (See Chapter 9.)
Programs	What programs are involved in the family–professional partnership?
	What do programs understand about how early intervention works?
	How will professionals collaborate with each other across programs?
	What needs to happen to get supports from different programs?
Partnership	Who are members of the family–professional partnership?
	How is the family participating in the partnership?
	How is the family–professional partnership collaborating?
	How are partnership members supporting each other's efforts?
	What is the easiest way to get needed resources?

- overseeing the family's early intervention program ("making sure early intervention happens the way it's supposed to");
- coordinating the family–professional partnership ("all the professionals are on the same page");
- supporting the family in getting and using resources both inside and outside of early intervention ("tell us which local child care providers have experience"); and
- meeting family outcomes ("helping us complete these forms").[1]

These service coordination tasks are described in more detail below.

Administrative Oversight. With each step in the early intervention process, there are rules to follow, forms to complete, and family rights to review. Service coordinators know these procedures, can explain them to the family–professional partnership, and ensure that each step of the process occurs as expected. Service coordinators facilitate and oversee the early intervention process to make sure it flows smoothly.[2]

Various funds are used to pay for early intervention supports and other resources, including government programs, private foundations, health insurance, and family fees. Use of these funds is essential so that each family gets the supports they expect. It is also important so that the early intervention system as a whole can continue. Service coordinators know how early intervention is funded and which sources pay for different early intervention supports.

Partnership Collaboration. When many programs and professionals are involved with a family, the family's priorities and the family's role as a partnership member might get lost. Service coordinators make sure that families are participating as an equal partner in the early intervention process and have a final say in the goals and supports they want from early intervention. In other words, "families are leading the collaborative process . . . [and] are active participants in the process, not consumers of a product."[3] Service coordinators, and all early intervention professionals, support families as they fulfill this role.

There are many different professionals from different specialties who might support families in early intervention. As described in Chapter 5, the main specialties are occupational therapy, physical therapy, speech-language pathology, and special instruction. Table 8.2 lists the other specialties early intervention must have available under the Individuals with Disabilities Education Act (IDEA). This list, however, does not mean that all families receive all these supports. And there might be other supports available by state, local, or private programs. Each family–professional partnership identifies those supports necessary to meet the family's priorities.

As stated in Chapter 5, all partnership members need to understand what everyone else is doing and learn from each other. The service coordinator makes sure that the team is working together so they complement (versus contradict) each other. Also, team members should not be doing the same thing, or duplicating each others' work. If that happens, the family–professional partnership comes together to create a new, more effective way to provide supports. When supports

Table 8.2. Additional Early Intervention Services Under Part C of IDEA

Resource	Specialty Focus†
Assistive Technology	Devices and services to evaluate, obtain, and use devices
Audiology Services	Hearing functioning
Family Training and Counseling	" [A]ssist the family . . . in understanding the special needs of the child and enhancing the child's development"‡
Health Services	As needed to benefit from other early intervention services; consultation to provide early intervention
Medical Services	Diagnosis and evaluation for early intervention eligibility
Psychological Services	Psychological and developmental testing, behavior analysis, and mental health
Sign- and Cued Language Services	Services for hearing impairments (listed under speech-language pathology)
Social Work	Social-emotional skills, parent–child interaction, and home environments
Transportation/ Related Costs	Cost of travel and similar costs for early intervention
Vision Services	Visual functioning, orientation, and mobility

† For a complete description according to Part C regulations (Federal Regulations for Early Intervention Program for Infants and Toddlers with Disabilities, 1999), see §303.13(b).
‡ Federal Regulations for Early Intervention Program for Infants and Toddlers with Disabilities, 1999, §303.13(b)(3)

are coordinated, each partnership member enhances the abilities of the other. The service coordinator is the point person who makes sure everyone is focused toward meeting the family's outcomes.

Resources Inside and Outside of Early Intervention. Early intervention as a program is not intended to meet all of a family's priorities. But, early intervention is supposed to support families in finding and getting any resources that help them meet their priorities. These resources can be a part of early intervention, or outside the specialized supports provided by early intervention. Service coordinators know what resources are available in the family's community, have connections with those resources, and support families in getting those resources.[4]

Just as the family–professional partnership works best when coordinated, so too do the community resources outside of early intervention. For example, as Kenisha Coles said, early intervention needs to know what Dionne's doctors are doing, and the doctors need to know what early intervention is doing. Service coordinators facilitate collaboration across resources inside and outside of early intervention. Most particularly, service coordinators make sure that all supports are working with the same information and are focused toward family priorities. For example, the early intervention family–professional partnership needs to know that the feeding team is working toward weaning Dionne off her feeding tube and how they plan to do that. The feeding team needs to know the progress the early intervention partnership has had around Dionne eating. Both teams need to share and coordinate their work. Service coordinators help families "get supports and services that are coordinated, effective, and individualized to meet [their] needs."[5]

Family Outcomes. As with child outcomes, the family–professional partnership decides on the best partnership member to support each family outcome. Sometimes, the service coordinator might take the lead in partnering with families to address family outcomes, most likely because of his or her knowledge of various resources. For example, Holly knows the different child care options available, how to get an AT evaluation, and how to enroll in the Children with Special Health Care Needs program. Therefore, Holly is the best partner member to support these outcomes. In some situations, team members share responsibility for family outcomes based on their areas of expertise. For example, Dionne's AT evaluation identified a particular chair that can help support Dionne when sitting. The family–professional partnership might decide that Holly can best assist the Coles-Williams family in completing the paperwork for this equipment. At the same time, Julio knows how to describe why the equipment is needed, and can best speak with the insurance company to make a case for covering the cost of the seat.

As illustrated in the examples, there are different ways to achieve the various tasks of service coordination—oversight, partnership coordination, resources, and family outcomes. The most appropriate ways are determined by each family–professional partnership.

The Family–Professional Partnership

Service coordination occurs in the same way that family–professional partnerships occur during home and community visits. The family–professional partnership identifies the family's specific service coordination priorities. These priorities are the service coordination responsibilities (processes, programs, and people) and tasks (oversight, partnership coordination, resources, and family outcomes). Then, the family and service coordinator bring together their strengths to meet the identified priorities. The service coordinator brings knowledge of early intervention procedures and outside resources, and the ability to facilitate collaboration among the family and professional partners. The family may also bring many of the same competencies. Depending on how long the family has been in early intervention, the family may be quite familiar with early intervention procedures. Each family will vary in their knowledge of outside resources and facilitation skills. Every family brings their vision of how they would like to participate in service coordination. Some families will want to take on virtually all service coordination responsibilities. Other families will utilize the service coordinator's strengths more often. The family–professional partnership identifies who will be responsible for which service coordination priorities. For example, Holly is taking the lead on some priorities—AT evaluation, child care, and Children with Special Health Care Needs program. There are other areas of coordination that Kenisha and Gary are handling. Kenisha coordinates with the medical equipment vendor to make sure they always have the necessary supplies. Gary coordinates the schedule of medical appointments. Each family–professional partnership decides how best to work together. The early intervention service coordinator is there to help the family as desired. The service coordinator does not replace families in what they see as their responsibility in parenting their child. When the family's service coordination priorities are met in a way that best supports the family, the expected results for service coordination can be achieved.

EXPECTATIONS OF SERVICE COORDINATION

What are the expected results of service coordination? A group of researchers have begun to figure that out.[6] They identified the following outcomes of effective service coordination:

> *Family obtains supports, information, and education to address their
> individual needs.* For example, the Carmina family is figuring out in-home
> child care through informal resources (see Chapter 3) while the Coles-

Williams family is figuring out child care that is best able to support Dionne's medical and learning characteristics.

Family communicates the needs of their child. This might occur *within* the family professional-partnership. For example, in Chapter 5, Kenisha and Gary clearly described Dionne's needs during the IFSP meeting, and continue to do this during intervention visits. Or, the family might communicate their child's needs to others *outside* of early intervention, such as the Carminas are doing with the support of early intervention.

Family makes informed decisions about services, resources, and opportunities for their child. In the examples, both families understand, value, and agree with the early intervention supports they receive and how their team works together.

Agencies and professionals are coordinated. This outcome is clearly being met for both families based on the way the family–professional partnerships team and coordinate with outside resources.

Child and family receive quality services. The service coordinators, Patrice and Sarah, continually check in with the families to make sure the families feel the supports are effective in meeting their priorities.

When these service coordination outcomes are met, early intervention is expected to better meet its overall goal of supporting families as they facilitate their child's learning and development.[7]

FORMAL COMMUNITY RESOURCES

There are many resources in a family's community, outside of early intervention, that can support the family in meeting their priorities. As stated previously, early intervention service coordinators know what those resources are, and the best ways to obtain them. Below are examples of potential community resources for families. Some are available to all families, while others are more specific to families of children with developmental delays or disabilities. These examples are separated into three types of resources—health, developmental, and family support resources.

Health Community Resources

Health resources help meet the child's medical and nutritional needs. Some health resources are common for many children. For example, all children need to see a primary doctor, such as a pediatrician or a general practitioner, as well as a dentist. And, all families benefit from having health insurance for their child. There are other resources that are more frequently used by families of children with special health care needs. These specialized supports can be medical specialists, such as Dionne's neurologist and ophthalmologist, as well as genetics doctors and developmental pediatricians. For children who are frequently in and out of the hospital, the family–professional partnership interacts and coordinates with the medical staff at the hospital. Local children's hospitals not only provide care for children when they stay at the hospital, but also provide expertise in the medical needs of children who do not stay there, such as the supports provided by Dionne's feeding team. Table 8.3 describes a variety of community resources available to meet children's health care needs.

Table 8.3. Health Community Resources

Resource	Supports Provided
Primary Care/Medical Home	Usual source of preventive and medical care who coordinates other medical and health resources
Dental	Oral health supports, including dentists who specialize in young children or children with disabilities
Private Health Insurance	Health care coverage families have through their place of employment or on their own
State Children's Health Insurance	Health care coverage provided by the state to children of families who are eligible (defined by the particular state)
Medicaid Insurance	Health care coverage for families/children who meet income requirements
Early Periodic Screening, Detection, and Treatment (EPSDT)	Part of Medicaid for children to identify (as early as possible) and address any physical, mental, developmental, dental, hearing, or vision concerns
Developmental Pediatrician	Medical doctors who specialize in children (i.e., pediatrics) and specifically developmental needs
Medical Specialists	Doctors who specialize in certain areas of health, such as cardiology, neurology, and pulmonary (breathing)
Nutrition	Supports for the family's dietary needs
Genetics	Supports for children and families with genetic-related needs, such as diagnostic evaluation, education and medical care, and genetic counseling
Children with Special Health Care Needs	Supports for families of children with special health care needs so the child's care is coordinated and community-based
Visiting Nurses	Home-based care to meet medical needs
Children's Hospitals	Medical centers specializing in the health care needs of children
Neonatal Intensive Care Unit Team	Professionals who provide intensive care in the hospital right after birth
Pediatric Intensive Care Unit Team	Professionals who provide intensive care when children are in the hospital

The Medical Home. All children benefit from having one place to go for non-specialized medical care—the place where the doctors are familiar with the family and what's important to their individual culture and family life. The doctors know the child well, including the child's medical history. There is typically one place the family goes for their child's well-baby checkups, immunizations, illnesses, and accidents. These professionals are usually primary care doctors who care for the child as the child grows up. Children who go to medical specialists and have multiple health care needs might see many doctors. They might see certain doctors for a little while, like a neonatologist or a surgeon. They might see other specialists for the entire time they are growing up, like an ear, nose and throat doctor. The more doctors a child sees, the more challenging it can be for families to follow all the advice provided. Recommendations from different doctors might contradict each other and might not match the family's cultural values.

As with a service coordinator, families benefit from having one person who organizes the child's records and coordinates health care information across doctors. This person, usually the child's primary care doctor, is called a *medical home* (see http://www.aap.org/healthtopics/medicalhome.cfm/). The medical home is responsible for making sure all the doctors communicate about their medical opinions and recommendations, that the recommendations across doctors make sense, and that they fit the particular family. The early intervention family–professional partnership can make sure that the child has a medical home, and that early intervention coordinates with the child's medical home so the child's health and developmental needs are well orchestrated.

Developmental Community Resources

While early intervention provides developmental supports specifically for children with developmental delays or disabilities, there are other community resources that focus on the development of all children. As discussed in Chapter 7, children with developmental delays or disabilities can also participate in these learning opportunities as members of the community. Table 8.4 describes possible developmental community resources available to families of young children.

Family Support Community Resources

As with medical and developmental resources, community resources that meet the priorities of families might be specifically for families with young children with developmental delays or disabilities, such as the parent-to-parent program Kenisha and Gary joined. Or, they might be for any interested family. Some family support resources might be for families of children with specific characteristics, but not necessarily only developmental delays or disabilities. For example, there are groups for families of children with autism or Down syndrome. But there are also

Table 8.4. Developmental Community Resources

Resource	Supports Provided
Infant–Toddler Playgroups, Gyms, and Classes	Various group activities for infants and toddlers based on the interests of the family and child
Child Care Resource and Referral	Local resource to identify child care that offers what a family wants from child care
Child Care Programs	Centers and family homes that provide out of home care and developmental supports to young children
Home Visiting Programs (e.g., Parents as Teachers, Nurse–Family Partnership)	Developmental programs that support family–child interaction and promote child development in the home (Note: There are different eligibility requirements for each program)
Head Start/Early Head Start	Home and center-based developmental and family support programs for families who are eligible based on income. Early Head Start is for pregnant women, and families of infants and toddlers; Head Start is for families of preschool-age children
General Preschool Programs	Public ("universal") and private programs for pre-kindergarten children to promote learning and development in group settings
Preschool Special Education Programs	Specialized supports provided to preschoolers who are eligible due to developmental delays or disabilities

groups for families of multiples, like the Simmons-Crause family want to find. Family community resources might be helpful in meeting family or parenting outcomes. Table 8.5 describes different kinds of community resources designed to support families.

As shown in Tables 8.3 through 8.5, there are many community resources outside early intervention. Service coordinators know about these resources. What is provided? Who is eligible? What is the easiest way to get these resources? Service coordinators also keep track of what other families thought of the resources they tried. What do other families say about the quality of this resource? Did the resource meet the family's needs? This can be useful information as the family–professional partnership decides whether to pursue specific resources or not. Early intervention programs can provide a current directory of community resources so the family–professional partnership has contact information to easily connect with a resource.

DIFFERENT PROGRAMS, DIFFERENT WAYS

So far, this chapter has focused on the kinds of resources and supports that are coordinated and the expected results of coordination. *Who* actually provides service

Table 8.5. Family Support Community Resources

Resource	Supports Provided
Family Resource Centers	Organizations, some general and some topic-focused, that provide parenting supports for health, developmental, educational, and safety needs
Family Centers	Community programs to support families
Parent to Parent Networks	Opportunities to connect with families with similar parenting circumstances through group or individual relationships (e.g., parents of multiples, specific disabilities, or infants/toddlers)
Mental Health	Counseling and other supports for positive emotional health
Military Families	Supports designed to meet the unique needs of families in the military
Education and Employment	Resources to access education and job opportunities for adult family members
Disability Specific Opportunities	Agencies and supports that are designed to meet the needs of families of children with disabilities, such as Parent Training and Information Centers, day camps, the ARC, and respite services
Charities	Local, state, and national assistance programs to meet families' needs, such as Goodwill and Habitat for Humanity
Women, Infants, Children (WIC)	Nutritional program for pregnant and nursing women, and children under the age of 5 years
Financial	Resources to assist with monetary needs, such as child support, financial assistance, and meeting basic needs
Social Services	Services to meet the basic health, safety, and care needs of families
Crisis Supports	Violence and other emergency supports

coordination will depend on the early intervention program. Service coordinators can be the same professional as the one providing developmental supports, like Patrice, the physical therapist, does for the Carmina family. Or, the service coordinator can be a professional whose sole role is to provide service coordination, like Holly. The service coordinator might be at the same agency as the early intervention team. Or, the service coordinator might be at a different agency. These are the primary ways state early intervention programs set up service coordination.[8]

However, early intervention programs might offer different service coordination options. For example, in some programs, the type of service coordination depends on the family's coordination needs. For a family with few early intervention supports and no special outside supports to speak of, like the Carminas, the early intervention professional would be the service coordinator. For families with many early intervention team members and outside supports, such as the Coles-Williamses, the family–professional partnership might decide that a professional who can focus only on service coordination responsibilities would work best. In other programs, service coordination responsibilities might be shared among professionals. For example, the early intervention professional might be responsible for coordinating the early intervention team and supporting the family in addressing family outcomes. At the same time, the service coordinator might be responsible for overseeing early intervention and making sure procedures are met. Another model might have one service coordinator who supports families as they enter early intervention, such as organizing the eligibility evaluation and initial IFSP development. Another person provides ongoing service coordination once the family is enrolled.

There is limited research on these different service coordination models. One published study looked at the three major models of service coordination—primary early intervention professional as service coordinator, separate service coordinator at the same agency, and separate service coordinator at a different agency. This study found that service coordinators who are not in the same agency as the early intervention service providers fulfilled fewer of the service coordination tasks (see "Pulling It All Together") than the other two types of service coordinators, and service coordinators who were also the primary early intervention professional saw family–professional partnership members more frequently than service coordinators who were not at the same agency.[9] It is expected that ongoing contact with families and professionals, and fulfilling service coordination tasks, are necessary to meet the expected outcomes of service coordination.[10] For example, if Holly didn't spend the amount of time she does with Kenisha, Gary, and the early intervention professionals, it would be difficult to meet all her responsibilities. Whatever model is used, the family–professional partnership can make sure that all of the family's service coordination priorities are being met and that the frequency with which service coordination occurs is enough to meet those priorities.

THE BIG PICTURE: RELATED POLICIES AND GUIDELINES

Service coordination is a specific service listed in IDEA. Service coordination must be provided at no cost to families. In IDEA legislation, the service coordinator is specifically identified as the person "who will be responsible for the implementation of the plan and coordination with other agencies and persons, including transition services."[11] In the federal regulations, service coordination services are expected to "assist and enable a child . . . and the child's family to receive the rights, procedural safeguards, and services that are authorized."[12] This includes:

- interagency coordination,
- access to and coordination of early intervention and other services,
- one contact person for coordinating evaluations and assessments,
- intervention planning, review, and evaluation,
- coordination and oversight of early intervention supports,
- information on families' rights,
- coordination of funding sources, and
- transition.[13]

The IDEA legislation reinforces the important role service coordination plays to ensure families can get and use desired supports in a way that works for them and is effective in meeting their child and family priorities.

SUMMARY: MAKING IT ALL MAKE SENSE

There are many steps to the early intervention process and multiple resources available to families. Making sense of it all requires coordination, however. The family–professional partnership coordinates supports and services so families can easily and successfully participate in early intervention the way it's supposed to happen, collaborate with professionals inside and outside of early intervention and get needed resources to meet their priorities. That way, families and children aren't pulled in separate directions. Instead, supports are pulled together.

Preparing for the Partnership: What Families Bring

The following questions can be considered by family members to prepare for participation in service coordination:

Oversight:
What questions do you have about early intervention procedures?
What questions do you have about your rights as an early intervention
    participant?
How will you know when service coordination is working for you? What will
    that look like?

Participation:
How would you like to participate in service coordination? How do you
    envision working with the service coordinator?
What questions do you have about how service coordination is provided?

Collaboration:
Who are the people and programs involved in your early intervention
    family–professional partnership? How do you envision the partnership
    coordinating their efforts?
Who are the people and programs involved with your family outside of early
    intervention? How do you envision the partnership coordinating with
    those outside resources?

Resources:
What health, developmental, or family support resources might be helpful to
    you?
How can the service coordinator support you in obtaining those resources?

Does your child have a successful medical home? What do you want from a medical home?

What questions do you have about how early intervention and other resources are funded? What are specific funding areas you would like to discuss with your service coordinator?

Preparing for the Partnership: What Professionals Bring

The following questions can be considered by early intervention professionals to prepare for participation in service coordination:

Oversight:

How will you explain service coordination, and your program's service coordination model, to the family? What else do you need to know so you can fully explain it to the family?

How will you explain early intervention procedures to the family? What else do you need to know so you can fully explain it to the family?

How will you explain the family's rights as an early intervention participant? What else do you need to know about their rights?

How will you know when certain service coordination outcomes are achieved?

Participation:

How will you support the family in identifying the way they want to participate in service coordination?

How will you support the family in their chosen role?

Collaboration:

Who are the people and programs involved in the early intervention family–professional partnership? How will you make sure efforts are coordinated?

Who are the people and programs involved with the family outside of early intervention? How will you make sure that the family–professional partnership coordinates with those outside resources?

Resources:

What do you know about various health, developmental, and family support resources? What else do you need to know?

What do you know about the procedures for obtaining various resources? How can you make connections with other resources?

What do you know about the concept of a medical home? What else do you need to know?

Does your program have a community resources directory?

What do you know about funding for early intervention and other resources? What else do you need to know?

Chapter 9

CONSIDERING NOW— AND LATER

The Cabreras talk about wanting Franco to grow up to be a happy child who takes care of others and thinks about the world around him. They want him to value family and their family's history. They want him and his brother to be the best of friends who can always count on each other.

The Liangs talk about Jia getting a good education, going to college, and making a difference in the world. They envision her being successful in school and in outside activities. They say Jia does not have to be the most popular girl in school, or have the most friends, but they want her to have those few special friends who understand and love her.

Kenisha Coles and Gary Williams talk about Dionne being a productive member of society, contributing in some way. They envision her being an active member of their church community and having a lot of friends. They want her to enjoy life and learning. And, they want her to know right from wrong as she makes decisions about her life.

Throughout the early intervention process, the family–professional partnership has kept the family's vision for their child at the forefront of all that happens. Those visions are not only what families want for their children as infants and toddlers. Families look into the future and think about what they want for their children as they grow up—how they see their child participating as a member of their family and community. It's what the family wants for their child as a preschooler, a school-age child, and as an adult. The future can feel very far off for families and professionals alike, especially when they are concerned about the child's current development. But, early intervention is just the beginning of the child's learning and participation in their home and community. What happens after early intervention? The family–professional partnership can think about this, by addressing the family's priorities of the present, as well as setting a positive course for the future.

EARLY INTERVENTION:
SETTING A POSITIVE COURSE FOR THE FUTURE

Research has shown that interventions for young children with developmental delays or disabilities can be effective in promoting learning and development.[1] While not all children leave early intervention developing as typically expected, early interventions can help children make more positive gains than they would without early intervention. Developmental leaders, however, also caution the use of interventions that ignore or even diminish the ordinary processes that facilitate child learning and development.[2] They caution about interventions that decrease parental competence, dismiss the family's culture and values, segregate children from natural learning opportunities, and result in families "interact[ing] with their child in an unnatural, therapeutic manner rather than through a natural and comfortable parent–child relationship."[3] While these interventions may result in the achievement of certain behaviors or skills, it may be at the expense of natural and future functioning. Instead, the family–professional partnership can take advantage of the natural way children develop while also considering the child's unique learning characteristics.

Therefore, the family–professional partnership considers both the competencies that the family wants the child to learn now, and how those competencies are learned to positively impact current learning, as well as learning in the near and later future. Of course, as children learn new developmental competencies they will be able to build on those competencies in future learning. The family–professional partnership, however, can think about what else the child is learning from interventions, and makes sure that it is positive and supportive of children learning, participating, and growing in the world around him or her. Consider the following:

- A family feels uncomfortable using strategies that prevent the child from moving the way the child does to get around. They do not want to disrupt the child's freedom to explore and learn on his own.
- A family puts Velcro on the child-sized play table and his toys so objects are stable and the child can use and explore them. That way, the child can more easily participate in play routine activities, which leads to learning.[4]
- An interventionist explains that the child's challenging behaviors (such as biting, hitting, and throwing tantrums) is the way he tells the family what he wants. The interventionist suggests that the family–professional partnership avoid simply stopping the challenging behaviors, but instead teach the child a new way to communicate.[5]
- The family–professional partnership identifies pictures for the child to communicate with and a walker to help move around. That way, the child has a successful way, or *form*, to achieve the expected competency, or *function* (see Chapter 2).[6]

- The family–professional partnership decides to interact with the child in positive ways when the child is already motivated to figure something out, but to save praise for when the child really needs outside encouragement to try. That way, the child learns a positive self-concept and pride in his or her accomplishments without external rewards.[7]

These are examples of how the family–professional partnership thinks about the influence of certain intervention strategies on the child's overall learning and development. In each of these examples, the family–professional partnership finds ways to promote learning and participation, which results in the child feeling understood and successful. Two concepts related to this are learning how to learn and self-determination.

Learning How to Learn

Throughout the chapters, various competencies that infants and toddlers can learn have been described. These competencies are the foundation to learning new competencies as the child grows up. They are the *what* of learning. There are also competencies and skills that the child uses in order to figure out, and learn, new competencies. These are the *how* of learning. During the infant–toddler years, children are beginning to learn ways to understand and figure out the world.[8] The foundational competencies emerging during infancy and toddlerhood are:

Paying attention: Children begin to learn that they have to pay attention to what they are doing, or what others are doing in order to figure things out. For example, if a child is not listening, or not paying attention, as a parent says words to imitate, the child wouldn't know what she or he is supposed to learn.

Persistence: Think about the old children's story about the "Little Engine That Could." It was teaching children about trying over and over again. Children can learn at an early age to keep trying.

Problem solving: Children begin to learn that trying different ways to accomplish a goal (that is, if one way doesn't work, try another) can lead to success. This can include trying different strategies, but also asking for help.[9]

Having a goal to achieve: The first stage of learning is simply exploring to learn about the characteristics of the world. But then, the child begins to explore in order to learn about how the child can affect the world.[10] At this stage, the child is trying to reach a specific goal he or she has in mind. The child is trying to figure out, or do, or obtain, or communicate something. When the child has a goal in mind, the child's learning is purposeful.

There are also emotional components to learning how to learn.[11] Learning needs to be enjoyable. If it's not, the child won't want to learn anymore. Children learn when they are excited about learning and want to figure things out. Children learn to feel good about their attempts, and when they are able to complete parts of goals, even if they don't complete the entire goal. And, of course, children feel good when the goal is finally met. The family–professional partnership can create interventions that focus on learning how to learn as well as what to learn.

Self-Determination

Consider the teenage years. During this time, teenagers are learning how to be adults. They make more and more of their own decisions—who they will hang out with, when they will do their homework or their chores, what they will do after high school. As families provide more opportunities for teenagers to make decisions, teenagers become more prepared for the "real world" as adults, and will have to make these decisions on their own. Teenagers are learning *self-determination—* the ability to take charge of one's life and make important life decisions.[12] Those who work with teenagers and young adults with disabilities have been thinking about how best to promote self-determination.[13] Just like any competency, children need opportunities to practice self-determination so they are ready to be self-determined when expected.

The early intervention field has begun thinking about what self-determination means to families in early childhood.[14] Clearly, young children, and certainly infants and toddlers, have fewer and less imperative decisions to make. There can be opportunities, however, to learn potential precursors to self-determination. Infant–toddler competencies that seem aligned with the idea of self-determination are:

- initiative (such as having toys within the child's reach so the child can decide when to play with what toy);
- choicemaking (such as which shirt to wear, which color cup to drink out of);
- regulation (such as controlling emotions and being able to handle the world around them); and
- problem solving, assertiveness, and persistence.[15]

However, the importance of these competencies can be different for each family based on their cultural values.[16] Therefore, the family–professional partnership can discuss how the family feels about these competencies, and how they can be integrated into their routine activities if the family values them. This idea of self-determination, or precursors to self-determination, in young children is in its early stages, and research is certainly needed.[17] Currently, there is no research that shows that promoting these competencies in young children results in more self-determined young adults. The family–professional partnership, however, can discuss these competencies and decide how to include them in early intervention based on the family's individual values and priorities.

Family Outcomes

While early intervention ends at 3 years of age, the family continues to parent the child—interacting and engaging the child, providing formal and informal learning opportunities, and providing for the child's care and safety needs.[18] The family will continue to make sure the child's developmental and educational programs meet the child's learning needs, and that other community and health resources help the family meet their priorities. The family will continue to have outcomes for their family as a whole, and individual family members. Early intervention professionals work with families so they are best prepared to meet their child and family priorities in the coming years. In early intervention, families learn about and link up with community resources they might not have even known about. They gain new competencies to be a voice for their child, such as the Carminas talking to others about Charlie's learning needs. The goal is not for families to leave early intervention ready to cope or "get by" without early intervention supports. Instead the goal of early intervention is for families and the community to no longer need early intervention. This occurs when families and the community can:

- promote the child's development because they understand the child's unique learning needs;
- advocate on the child's behalf when entering and participating in new programs, supports, and experiences; and
- connect to supports the family wants to meet their goals for their child and their family.

With these abilities, families are ready to move ahead without early intervention supports.

EARLY INTERVENTION TRANSITIONS

As described in Chapter 3, changes naturally occur in families.[19] Babies are born, children go to school, and adult children might move away. Families might move into new houses. New jobs could be acquired. Parents might decide to go back to work or school. With each change, families plan and prepare so that the change, or *transition*, to the new way of life goes smoothly. In early intervention, transitions to different places or programs also happen. Transitions occur when entering early intervention, during early intervention, and leaving early intervention. With each transition, the family–professional partnership plans out how the transition will occur. That way, the child and the family are ready. Let's look at each of these times of transition a little closer:

Where Are Families Before Early Intervention?

Jia Liang spent the first few weeks of her life in the Neonatal Intensive Care Unit (NICU). During her stay, her family partnered with the NICU staff so they were ready to care for Jia at home. They learned how to give Jia her medication, feed her, and what to look for if there were any concerns with her heart. Before she came home, the Liangs, the NICU staff, and the community early intervention program created the Individualized Family Service Plan (IFSP) so early intervention could begin as soon as the family got home. That way, there wasn't a wait before the family had the specialized supports they wanted.

For some families like the Liangs, the transition into early intervention is from one specialized support program, the NICU, into another, early intervention. For other families like the Carminas, the transition is from no specialized support program into early intervention. Either way, the family–professional partnership can make sure that families are supported as soon as possible and get into early intervention as easily as possible.

What Transitions Happen in Early Intervention?

The Coles-Williams family is getting ready for Dionne to begin child care. They have chosen a family child care home where a woman cares for two other young children. Dionne will be the only child with special needs. They chose this child care option because the woman is a retired nurse, and has raised four children of her own, including one with special health care needs. The Coles-Williams family has visited the child care home a few times, and Dionne seems to be comfortable there. The intervention plan has been revised, with the child care provider participating, so some intervention visits can occur at child care. The Coles-Williams family introduced the early intervention professionals to the child care provider.

In addition to this new child care arrangement, Dionne's medical status still results in some stays at the hospital, although they are less frequent and for shorter amounts of time. During the times at the hospital, Holly, the service coordinator, works with Kenisha and Gary to see if early intervention can support them in any way (that is, family and parenting outcomes), and if the hospital staff needs any information from early intervention. When Dionne is ready to leave the hospital, the early intervention family–professional partnership follows up with Dionne's pediatrician (that is, her medical home) to make sure the family–professional partnership knows all they need to know before intervention visits resume again.

Once families are in early intervention, transitions can still occur. Children may enter child care programs or other community activities. There can be unpredictable transitions, such as Dionne going to the hospital. Or, there can be regularly scheduled transitions, such as from home to childcare and back home again. Some children have two homes they transition between during the week. And for some families, the transition is from one early intervention program to another, such as when a family moves to a different early intervention jurisdiction. The family–professional partnership makes sure that each transition during early intervention—whether new, a regular occurrence, or unexpected—are at least coordinated and at best purposely planned and prepared for.

Where Do Families Go After Early Intervention?

Franco Cabrera's third birthday is coming sooner than his family can believe. At that point, the Cabrera family will no longer be eligible for early intervention. They are pretty sure Franco will be eligible for preschool special education. His family would like to keep the family's routine, and Franco's in particular, the same as possible, including staying at his child care center. When Franco turns 4 years old, they would like him to go to the public preschool program provided by the school district for all children.

Right now, families participating in early intervention programs funded by the Individuals with Disabilities Education Act (IDEA) transition out of early intervention no later than the child's third birthday. Some families leave early intervention prior to the age of 3 years. For example, the family–professional partnership may decide that early intervention is no longer needed. Just like during early intervention, the family–professional partnership plans and prepares for the transition out of early intervention. Some families will be eligible for specialized supports for children with developmental delays or disabilities. These are preschool programs under the auspices of special education. Other families will not be eligible for this program based on their child's current developmental functioning. In these situations, the family–professional partnership may choose other programs to support their child's developmental needs, such as group programs like private preschools, Head Start, or public preschools, sometimes called *universal* preschools because all children can attend them. Some children, while not eligible for public preschool special education, could still benefit from developmental supports and participate in private therapies paid for by insurance or the family. Or, the family–professional partnership may decide that the child will participate in home and community activities to continue learning and developing within everyday life. (Note: While some families may not use any type of program after early intervention, the term *program* is used for the rest of the chapter for simplicity.)

Most preschool programs, including preschool special education, are different from early intervention. The focus changes from family supports to child supports.[20] What's so special about the age of 3 years? Actually, the transition at 3 years is more of a function of the way programs are designed than any real developmental change in needs.[21] Some states start preschool special education earlier than 3 years, and some states and programs, for preschool special education, provide family supports. In fact, the current IDEA legislation[22] allows state early intervention programs to continue to provide supports to families eligible for preschool special education instead of having to transition to preschool. Regardless of whether the child is eligible for preschool special education, the family–professional partnership collaborates to create a plan that ensures a smooth transition out of early intervention.

PLANNING FOR AND CARRYING OUT TRANSITIONS

Roberto and Kat Cabrera explained to the preschool special education program that they wanted to keep Franco in his current child care center. Early intervention has already been providing supports there, and the child care teachers are ready to partner with the school system professionals in the same way. Since the Cabreras were hoping to enroll Franco in the universal preschool when he turned 4 years old, they didn't want him to change programs at 3 and then again at 4. The school system agreed to this arrangement, and planned for the preschool professionals who would be working with Franco in child care to go with the early intervention professionals on child care visits. That way, they can get to know the child care teachers and how interventions are already happening.

Transitioning out of early intervention can be an anxious time for families.[23] There are new members joining the family–professional partnership who need to get to know the family and the child. Old partnership members are leaving. How does one know when a transition is successful? It is when the family has the supports necessary to meet their goals and visions for their child's learning and development at this new point in their life. This occurs when transitions are planned, which begins by asking two questions:

1. What does the family–professional partnership need to do to get ready for the transition?
2. What does the child need in order to be ready for the transition?

There are many ways early intervention and preschool programs can collaborate so that families can smoothly transition from one program to another.[24] We will focus on the activities of the family–professional partnership. Creating a plan for transition can be just like creating an intervention plan. The family–professional partnership can identify child and family outcomes related to transition, as well as steps and approaches to meet these outcomes based on the family's values, priorities, and expectations of future programs.

Family transition outcomes may center on becoming informed about how transitions occur, and on specific characteristics about the program options available, including what's provided, how it's provided, and who's eligible.[25] For the Cabrera family–professional partnership, this conversation began well before the school system was involved. The service coordinator knew about the options available through preschool special education—an inclusive half-day preschool classroom, a half-day classroom only for children with developmental delays or disabilities, and itinerant supports who consult with families at home and professionals in typical early childhood programs. Another outcome for the Cabrera family was to be able to confidently describe their expectations and desires for Franco to remain in his current child care center.[26]

Child transition outcomes can focus on the competencies the child can learn while in early intervention so that the child is prepared to be successful in the new program.[27] These readiness skills might focus on playing with others, following routines, and/or controlling emotions. While Franco is staying at the same child care, he will be moving up to the 3-year-old classroom with his classmates. Therefore, all of the children in the class are learning the competencies expected for young children entering the preschool class. Since the early intervention family–professional partnership has always included Franco's child care teachers in the planning process, these kinds of outcomes were already a part of the intervention plan. For all child outcomes, the family–professional partnership focuses on generalizing the learning competencies across routine activities (see Chapter 2). That way, the child will know how to generalize the competencies to the new program.[28] Child transition outcomes can also focus on the child becoming familiar with the new program. The child can spend some time in the new program, paired with the child's parents or early intervention professionals. That way, the child gets to know the program's routines and the professionals who will be interacting with him or her.

Transition is a time to build new relationships. The family–professional partnership can meet with the new professionals, share information about the child and family, and visit new programs.[29] They can share what works well with the child as well as the child's strengths and needs. There will inevitably be some differences between any two programs, since one is for infants and toddlers and one is for preschoolers. However, there should be a level of similarity across programs because all quality programs focus on the way young children learn and develop.[30]

Some families feel a sense of loss leaving early intervention, and can be dissatisfied with preschool options, with the change in focus. However, if early intervention is done well, the family leaves early intervention more knowledgeable and ready to partner with this new environment—with the knowledge and skills to achieve their parenting outcomes. From the beginning, early intervention supports families to prepare for transition. At the end, when early intervention is done well, families know:

- their child's strengths and needs;
- how to advocate for their child;
- program options for preschool; and
- family support needs.[31]

TRANSITIONING TO INCLUSIVE ENVIRONMENTS

For children who continue to exhibit developmental delays or disabilities at preschool age, the family–professional preschool partnership will decide on the type of supports best for the child. According to IDEA, children are supposed to receive special education supports in the "least restrictive environment."[32] The term *least restrictive environments* means the most typical places where the child can be successful in learning, when appropriate supports are provided.

Years of research have shown that children with developmental delays or disabilities can successfully participate in regular preschool programs alongside typically developing children, known as *inclusion*.[33] However, this is not to say that children with developmental delays or disabilities can simply be placed in typical settings. They still need the specialized supports provided through special education. But, just like in home and community settings for infants and toddlers, preschool age children do not need to go to different places. What they need are individualized and specific approaches that help them actively participate and learn in preschool.[34] For that to happen, the teachers in those settings must be confident and competent in facilitating the child's learning and development based on his or her individual learning characteristics. As with Franco Cabrera, special education professionals can work in typical preschool settings so the teachers have the proper supports. Therefore, while early intervention can work on competencies to prepare the child for success in preschool, inclusive preschool programs also need to be prepared to support all children's learning strengths, needs, and characteristics. The transition plan and subsequent preschool special education supports can help preschool teachers prepare for and support children with developmental delays and disabilities to learn and participate in their programs.

THE BIG PICTURE: RELATED POLICIES AND GUIDELINES

The importance of planning for transition is clearly spelled out in the IDEA legislation and federal regulations.[35] For all children, the IFSP, or intervention plan, must include a transition plan, outlining how the family–professional partnership will prepare for the transition. This plan includes: "discussions with . . . parents regarding future placements and other matters related to the child's transition [and] procedures to prepare the child for changes in service delivery, including steps to help the child adjust to, and function in, a new setting." [36] Therefore, the responsibility of the family–professional partnership, and the service coordinator specifically, is to make sure that any new supports are in place when the child turns 3 years old.

The legislation and regulations specify many activities, with stated deadlines, for early intervention and preschool special education programs to meet around transitioning children into preschool special education. These activities include convening a meeting to plan the transition and, if the family wants, inviting an early intervention professional to the first preschool intervention planning meeting. While these guidelines are particularly for children who are eligible for preschool special education, the legislation also recognizes that families and children who are not eligible for special education are still experiencing a change. Therefore, early intervention professionals are required to create a transition plan with all families. However, IDEA cannot mandate that preschool programs outside of special education participate in transition practices. Therefore, the legislation *encourages* early intervention programs to try to coordinate with other preschool programs to plan transitions. Transitions can be confusing in that, one day a child is receiving early intervention supports that look a certain way (for example, twice a week at home) and the next day, these supports could look completely different (for example, 5 half-days a week in a classroom). This is usually a condition of the program versus the child. The child's needs didn't change simply because the child was 1 day older. Therefore, IDEA regulations stipulate that, when the first preschool supports are designed, the child's IFSP, or intervention plan, needs to be considered.

SUMMARY: CONSIDERING NOW—AND LATER

Early intervention provides supports during the initial years of parenting. The family–professional partnership can set a positive course of development by taking advantage of the natural way children develop while also considering the child's unique learning characteristics. To ensure smooth transitions into, during, and out of early intervention, the family–professional partnership can identify outcomes and plan ways to meet those outcomes so families and children are prepared.

Preparing for the Partnership: What Families Bring

Families can consider the following questions to prepare for setting a positive course of development and planning transitions:

Setting a Positive Course of Development:

What do you envision for your child at different ages? How can that vision be used in early intervention?

What competencies do you value for your child? How is early intervention promoting those competencies?

What questions do you have about using natural ways to promote child development?

What questions do you have about learning how to learn or self-determination? What do you think of these concepts?

Transitions:

What do you and your child need to prepare for transition into or out of early intervention?

What transitions might occur while in early intervention? How can early intervention help plan for those transitions?

What supports do you envision for your child after early intervention ends? Where do you envision your child will spend the day during the preschool years? What do you think your child needs to be successful there?

What questions do you have about the different support options after early intervention?

What do you need to meet your family and parenting outcomes in the future, after early intervention?

Preparing for the Partnership: What Professionals Bring

Professionals can consider the following questions to prepare for setting a positive course of development and planning transitions:

Setting a Positive Course of Development:

How will you come to know the family's vision for their child after early intervention? How will you use that information?

How do you ensure that interventions promote child competencies valued by the family?

How do you use natural ways of promoting child development?

What do you know about learning how to learn and self-determination? What else do you need to know? How will you understand the family's values around these ideas?

Transition:

How will you uncover the family's transition outcomes for themselves and their child?

What do you need in order to effectively partner with the family to prepare for transitions?

What do you know about the rules and regulations for transition planning and the transition process? What else do you need to know?

What do you know about the different preschool program options in the communities you support?

What have been effective approaches to supporting families to prepare for transitions?

How will you follow-up with the family after transition?

Chapter 10

FAMILY–PROFESSIONAL PARTNERSHIPS GOING FORWARD

Families with infants and toddlers who have developmental delays or disabilities can benefit from supports from professionals who understand their children's developmental strengths and needs. Families of children with special needs, like all families, provide opportunities for learning. Early intervention strives to fit specialized supports into the lives families have created for themselves. Early intervention does this by understanding each family's beliefs, values, and priorities and taking advantage of the natural learning opportunities that reflect these priorities. A strong family–professional partnership is needed to achieve this outcome. As stated in the Introduction, *The Early Intervention Guidebook* intends to illustrate to families and professionals current research, policy, practical literature, and recommended practices for early intervention, presented in a way so all members of the family–professional partnership can use it in their day-to-day interactions.

This book describes six concepts that guide how early intervention happens. These concepts are:

- Children learn and develop using their curiosity, active discovery, and genuine excitement in the everyday experiences that occur in their family and community.
- Children are part of a family. The goals, values, and needs of the family are the goals, values, and needs of the child.
- Children learn through the kinds of interactions they have with others and the objects they have to explore.
- Families and communities provide many learning opportunities for young children. Early intervention is a support to families and communities, not a substitute.
- There are multiple resources available for families, but accessing and organizing them will require coordination.

- Early intervention is just the beginning. As supports are provided in the present, the future is also considered.

Using these concepts, the family–professional partnership supports families to meet their parenting goal of helping their children learn and develop as the family envisioned they would. The purpose of early intervention is not to change or add to what families already want or do with their children. Instead, the objective is to understand the family's vision for their child as part of their family and community, and help the family achieve that vision.

These concepts and practices are recognized as the foundation for early intervention by family and professional leaders in the field. Not all early intervention supports occur this way, however. As discussed in the Introduction, early intervention professionals are not always trained to work with families as partners. They are more prepared to work directly with children. Similarly, families may hear about or assume that early intervention is about direct services to children. By illustrating early intervention in action, this book aims to match what's happening in early intervention practice to what's expected by early intervention leadership. While each family and early intervention plan is individualized and looks different, the general criteria for early intervention and how it occurs is the same for all family–professional partnerships. With this information, families and professionals can take action to make sure that early intervention happens the way it's supposed to happen. Readers are encouraged to expect early intervention to occur this way, and question when it doesn't. Together, the family–professional partnership can explore the concepts in this book, and determine how their early intervention partnership meets these expectations, and ways early intervention can be improved. When certain areas are not reflected, the family–professional partnership can brainstorm ways to aligned with recommended practices.

In addition to one's own early intervention partnership, families and professionals can support others as they strive to meet these expectations. Families can share this information with other families to use in their partnerships. Professionals can support other professionals at their program or agency. Both families and professionals can advocate for these practices with those who create and manage early intervention systems and legislation. They can encourage policies and procedures that make possible and expect early intervention to happen this way. This can occur at local early intervention programs, the state agency in charge of administering early intervention, and/or the federal government—those who make the laws and oversee them.

While the overarching early intervention concepts are expected to remain the same, specific models and implementation methods are constantly evolving. Research continues to occur, moving the field forward. Policies are updated, which change expectations for the family–professional partnership. For example, in the Individuals with Disabilities Education Act (IDEA) reauthorization in 2004, states were given the option to provide early intervention supports beyond the required age of 3 years, until the child is 5 years old.[1] This option is only for those children who would be eligible for preschool special education through the school system. This was not part of previous legislation. Families and professionals are encouraged to keep up-to-date on these developments. The resources in the appendices provide ways to help stay current and find allies in promoting effective early intervention. Families and professionals can support each other, and support other families and professionals, to meet the goals of early intervention. When this occurs, early intervention can achieve its goal—for families and their young children to learn, live, and grow by participating in home and community life as they envision it.

Appendix A

FAMILY–PROFESSIONAL PARTNERSHIP CHECKLISTS

FAMILY–PROFESSIONAL PARTNERSHIP: ASSESSMENT CHECKLIST (CHAPTER 4)

Family Vision: The family's vision and priorities are identified and used to shape assessments:

- ❏ The family identifies their priorities for their child's development based on 1.) the child's developmental competencies, 2.) the family's values, and 3.) the family's cultural expectations.
- ❏ The family identifies their priorities for their child's development based on 1.) the child's developmental concerns, 2.) the child's developmental strengths, and 3.) the family's vision of how they want to parent.
- ❏ The family identifies their priorities with guidance from early intervention professionals.
- ❏ The family's priorities are shaped into specific outcomes tailored to the unique characteristics of the child and family.
- ❏ The family's vision and priorities are used to shape assessments.

Assessment Methods: Assessments are conducted to create an authentic picture of the child's learning and development.

- ❏ Assessments occur in the family's routine activities as they usually happen.
- ❏ Assessments occur in multiple routine activities.
- ❏ Multiple assessment methods are used.
- ❏ The limitations of traditional assessments are considered when making early intervention decisions.

Assessment Components: Various child and environmental characteristics are assessed to ensure an authentic picture of the child's learning and development.

- ❏ Assessments identify the child's strengths and needs.
- ❏ Assessments identify the child's competencies as she or he uses them in everyday life.

❑ Assessments discover the influence of important people and particular places on the child's participation, learning, and development.
❑ Assessments uncover strategies that 1.) are already being used, 2.) have already been tried, and 3.) are potential strategies to test out.

Collaboration: The family–professional partnership works together so that multiple perspectives and opinions are obtained and used in assessment decisions.

❑ The purpose behind the assessments (that is, eligibility, planning interventions, how well an intervention is working) is clearly understood by all members of the partnership.
❑ All members of the partnership participate in planning the assessment.
❑ The roles and responsibilities of each member of the partnership are discussed and defined so that all are comfortable with their roles.
❑ The knowledge and expertise of both the family and professionals are used in the assessment.
❑ The observations, views, and perspectives of all partnership members are used and pooled to create a clear picture of the child's development.

FAMILY–PROFESSIONAL PARTNERSHIP:
PLANNING EARLY INTERVENTION SUPPORTS CHECKLIST
(CHAPTER 5)

What and Why: The family-professional partnership identifies appropriate outcomes, steps, and approaches for addressing family priorities.

- ❑ All of the family's priorities have an outcome.
- ❑ Outcomes span developmental domains.
- ❑ Outcomes specify particular routine activities or are described to span routine activities.
- ❑ All partnership members understand the outcomes and steps, including when they will be achieved.
- ❑ Learning strategies strengthen the child's strengths and address the child's needs across domains.
- ❑ Approaches consider the strengths and culture of the family.

Where and When: The family-professional partnership determines the location and frequency of intervention visits.

- ❑ All routine activities in different locations (for example, home, child care, community) are considered potential options for intervention visits.
- ❑ Intervention visits occur during the same routine activities where the family will use the learning strategies.
- ❑ All partnership members actively participate in intervention visits.
- ❑ Intervention visits occur frequent enough so the family feels supported in making decisions and using the approaches to meet their outcomes.
- ❑ Intervention visits occur just frequently enough so that the family is neither left without supports when needed nor begins to doubt their own abilities.
- ❑ The frequency of intervention visits consider 1.) the newness and complexity of strategies, 2.) the comfort and learning style of the family, and 3.) how frequently strategies might change.

Who and How: The family-professional partnership identifies its members and the way they will work together.

- ❑ All family and community partnership members are identified.
- ❑ Specific professional partnership members are chosen based on their expertise and fit.
- ❑ The way the family-professional partnership members will work with one another is specifically described. The professional partnership members are identified as direct or consultation supports.
- ❑ All professional members are responsible for all outcomes across domains.

Purposeful Planning: The family-professional partnership collaborates to create a meaningful intervention plan.

- ❑ The intervention plan is realistic and reflective of the family's desires.
- ❑ Family members actively participate in intervention planning. The family has the supports (for example, friends or other contacts, translators) needed to fully participate.
- ❑ The intervention plan is frequently revisited and fine-tuned as needed so the plan fits the family and the child.
- ❑ All family and professional partnership members are able to share their thoughts and ideas.

FAMILY–PROFESSIONAL PARTNERSHIP: INTERVENTION VISITS CHECKLIST (CHAPTER 6)

Collaboration: The family–professional partnership fully collaborates.

- ❑ All team members understand how early intervention works and collaborate in this way.
- ❑ The family members and professional members of the intervention partnership feel they can communicate openly and honestly.
- ❑ The family–professional partnership uses both the professional's and family's strengths to identify and fine-tune intervention strategies.
- ❑ Visits are flexible to accommodate family priorities, including rescheduling visits or changing visits to the times when different routine activities occur.

Natural Learning Strategies: The family–professional partnership makes sure the strategies fit the child and the family.

- ❑ Strategies are practiced during the intervention visit in the routine activities where the family will use the strategies.
- ❑ Intervention visits occur at the same time the routine activities usually occur.
- ❑ Strategies are embedded into routine activities.
- ❑ Strategies are easy for the family to use in between intervention visits.
- ❑ Strategies are implemented without professional assistance.
- ❑ Any materials used during the intervention visit remain with the family to use in between visits.
- ❑ Strategies are functional *and* created to provide multiple opportunities for practice.
- ❑ Strategies make sure that the child is actively participating.
- ❑ The strategies promote child interest, engagement, and just enough of a challenge.

Family Competence and Confidence: Intervention visits are structured so that the family feels comfortable and able to use the strategies in between visits.

- ❑ All members of the family–professional partnership *understand* how the strategies will help meet the family's outcomes.
- ❑ During professional *demonstrations* (modeling), the family is actively involved in learning the strategy.
- ❑ The family has an *opportunity to try out* the strategies during the intervention visit.
- ❑ The family *provides feedback* on how they feel about the strategies.
- ❑ All the family's questions or concerns about the strategies are addressed.
- ❑ The professional *provides feedback* on the family's use of the strategies.
- ❑ There are methods in place to keep track of whether the interventions are working.

FAMILY–PROFESSIONAL PARTNERSHIP: COMMUNITY VISITS CHECKLIST (CHAPTER 7)

(Also use the Chapter 6 checklist with community visits)

Community Interventions: The family–professional partnership plans and implements community interventions.

❏ The family–professional partnership has a plan if community members ask about the interventionist.
❏ Coaching in the community feels comfortable for the family, professional, and community members.
❏ Strategies fit the community routine activities in which the child participates.
❏ Community appropriate strategies are used (that is, the family feels comfortable using strategies in the community).
❏ Intervention strategies promote community membership.

Community Member Participation: The family–professional partnership includes and/or collaborates with community members.

❏ All necessary community members understand how early intervention works.
❏ All necessary community members are a part of intervention planning.
❏ All necessary community members participate in interventions.
❏ The family is informed and is a part of decision making for interventions occurring in child experiences.

FAMILY–PROFESSIONAL PARTNERSHIP:
SERVICE COORDINATION CHECKLIST
(CHAPTER 8)

Oversight: The service coordinator oversees the early intervention process.

- ❑ The service coordinator makes sure that early intervention happens the way it's expected.
- ❑ The family knows their rights and what to expect at each step of the early intervention process.
- ❑ Early intervention rules and procedures are followed at each step of the early intervention process.
- ❑ Family outcomes are being addressed in a way that fits the family's culture and way of life.

Participation: The family–professional partnership works in a way that the family leads the partnership.

- ❑ Family members are active participants in each step of the early intervention process. Professional partnership members support family members as active participants.
- ❑ Family members have the final say in the goals and supports they want from early intervention. Professional partnership members support families in their decisions for their family.

Collaboration: The family–professional partnership collaborates so that all team members are focused on meeting the family's priorities.

- ❑ All early intervention professionals are working toward the same goals.
- ❑ All partnership members are working with the same information.
- ❑ The service coordinator facilitates collaboration across supports inside and outside of early intervention.
- ❑ The service coordinator makes sure the team members are working together so they complement each other.
- ❑ The service coordinator makes sure that multiple team members are not doing the same thing or contradicting each other.

Resources: The family–professional partnership makes sure the family has the necessary resources inside and outside of early intervention to meet the family priorities.

- ❑ The service coordinator connects the family with resources in the family's community.
- ❑ The family is getting and using the desired early intervention resources.
- ❑ The family is getting and using the desired community resources.
- ❑ The family has a medical home for their child and is comfortable and happy with their child's medical home.
- ❑ The family–professional partnership accesses the necessary funds to pay for early intervention and other resources.

FAMILY–PROFESSIONAL PARTNERSHIP:
POSITIVE COURSE OF DEVELOPMENT AND TRANSITIONS CHECKLIST
(CHAPTER 9)

Positive Course of Development: The family–professional partnership sets a positive course of development through early intervention.

❑ Strategies used are effective in promoting current competencies as well as positively influencing the child's developmental course.
❑ The family–professional partnership discusses learning how to learn and self-determination. These ideas are used in interventions as appropriate to the family's values and priorities.
❑ The family–professional partnership discusses the family's future role in parenting their child as the child grows up. There are family outcomes that prepare the family for this role.

Transitions: The family–professional partnership plans for transitions into, during, and out of early intervention.

❑ The family easily and quickly transitions into early intervention. Early intervention coordinates with other programs to ensure a smooth transition.
❑ The family–professional partnership identifies if there are any transitions occurring, or potentially occurring, while the family is in early intervention. There is a plan for these transitions.
❑ There is a plan for transitions out of early intervention, including child and family transition outcomes.
❑ There is a plan for informing the family about their options after early intervention ends.
❑ The family–professional partnership addresses child competencies so the child is successful in future programs.
❑ The transition plan includes familiarizing the child with new professionals and programs.
❑ The plan considers ways to support the family in discussing their child's strengths and needs, and advocating for their child.
❑ The plan includes linking the family to resources to meet future family and parenting outcomes after transition.

Appendix B

ACRONYMS

This appendix serves as a quick reference guide to acronyms included in the book and used in early intervention practice.

AT: Assistive Technology

DEC: Division for Early Childhood, Council for Exceptional Children

ECO: Early Childhood Outcomes (Center)

IDEA: Individuals with Disabilities Education Act

IFSP: Individualized Family Service Plan

NAEYC: National Association for the Education of Young Children

NICU: Neonatal Intensive Care Unit

OSEP: Office of Special Education Programs

Appendix C

DEFINITIONS

This appendix serves as a quick reference guide to terminology included in the book and used in early intervention practice.

Adaptive Development. The use and development of self-help skills for everyday needs, such as bathing, toileting, dressing, and safety.

Affective Development. See social-emotional development.

Assessment. Procedures used to understand a child's development in order to plan interventions and determine the effectiveness of interventions.

Authentic Assessments—Assessing child learning and development in the routine activities of the child's everyday life.

Assistive Technology. Any material that is added to a routine activity or modified that makes it easier for a child to participate and learn.

Cognitive Development. The use and development of mental capacities or thinking, such as problem solving, and learning concepts such as colors, size, and shapes.

Communication Development. The use and development of various ways to communicate.

Expressive Communication—Conveying one's thoughts and feelings through words, gestures, body language, and/or communication devices.

Receptive Communication—Understanding what others are trying to communicate.

Developmental Delay. When a child is developing at a slower pace than usually expected, or a child's developmental course is different than typically expected. The specific definition of developmental delay is defined differently by each state early intervention program.

Disciplines. Various professional specialties that provide early intervention services. The primary disciplines in early intervention are occupational therapy, physical therapy, special instruction, and speech-language pathology.

Early Intervention. Programs designed for families of infants and toddlers (up to 36 months) with or at risk for developmental delays or disabilities to help families set a positive course for their child's development.

Engagement. Active participation in routine activities in a way that makes sense for the child and activity.

Established Condition. A medical or developmental diagnosis that, according to a
   state's eligibility definition, results in automatic eligibility for early intervention
   regardless of whether the child has a developmental delay.
Evaluation. Procedures used to determine eligibility for early intervention.
Individualized Family Service Plan (IFSP). The written plan developed to 1.) identify
   the child and family outcomes expected to be achieved, and 2.) outline how
   early intervention will support the family in achieving those outcomes.
   Concerns, Priorities, and Resources—Part of the IFSP where the family's
      hopes, dreams, and needs for their particular family, their child, and any
      other family members are described. Concerns and priorities make up the
      outcomes of the IFSP. Resources are the strengths the family already has
      to meet the outcomes, and the family–professional partnership can build
      upon in early intervention.
   Outcomes—Identified in the IFSP as the expected results of participating
      in early intervention. Outcomes can be related to child learning and
      development (child outcomes) or family priorities and needs (family
      outcomes).
Individuals with Disabilities Education Act (IDEA), Part C. The federal legislation
   enacting early intervention for families with infants and toddlers with or at
   risk for developmental delays and disabilities.
Motor Development. The use and development of muscles for movement,
   positioning, and manipulation.
   Fine Motor—Use and development of the small muscles in the hands and
      mouth, such as grasping objects, scribbling, using mealtime utensils, and
      chewing.
   Gross Motor—Use and development of the large muscles in the arms and legs,
      such as reaching, throwing, crawling, walking, or running.
Natural Environments. The routine activities of the child's everyday life in the
   home and community where early intervention supports are provided.
Neonatal Intensive Care Unit (NICU). The special care nursery unit of a hospital
   where newborns with medical needs are cared for.
Occupational Therapy/Therapist. Services and professionals who specialize in
   fine motor development. In early intervention, however, these professionals
   can address all areas of development with support from other professional
   disciplines.
Office of Special Education Programs (OSEP). The federal agency in the U.S.
   Department of Education responsible for administering and overseeing the
   implementation of Part C early intervention programs.
Physical Environment. The objects (such as toys, tools, and furniture), the layout,
   and the sights and sounds of the routine activity that can be modified to create
   positive learning opportunities.

Physical Therapy/Therapist. Services and professionals who specialize in gross motor development. In early intervention however, these professionals can address all areas of development with support from other professional disciplines.

Regulation. Coping with sensations or changes in one's environment, known as *stressors.* These stressors can be internal to the child, such as being hungry or tired, or can come from outside the child, such as loud noises or meeting strangers.

Responsive Interactions. An adult understands a child's signals or cues and answers, or responds to the child, according to what the child is trying to say.

Routine Activities. What children do as they participate in their home and community life where opportunities for learning and development occur.

Service Coordination/Coordinator. Services and professionals responsible for overseeing and organizing the early intervention process.

Social-Emotional. The development of and ability to express feelings and interact with others.

Social Environment. The important people in a routine activity who interact with the child and can create positive learning opportunities.

Special Instruction/Special Instructor (also known as Special Education/ Special Educator). Services and professionals who specialize in the cognitive and social-emotional processes of development and disabilities. In early intervention, however, these professionals can address all areas of development with support from other professional disciplines.

Speech Therapy/Speech-Language Pathologist. Services and professionals who specialize in communication development. In early intervention, however, these professionals can address all areas of development with support from other professional disciplines.

Transition Plan. A description of the steps to be completed so that a family and child can successfully move into or out of specific programs, services, or supports.

Appendix D

RESOURCES

Below are various organizations whose Web sites have informational resources for families and professionals.

American Academy of Pediatrics

www.aap.org   847–434–4000

Professional association for pediatricians. Resources on the health and development of young children specifically for pediatricians but also families and other professionals.

American Association for Home-Based Early Interventionists (AAHBEI)

www.aahbei.org   800–396–6144

Membership association for parents and professionals involved in home-based services.

American Physical Therapy Association (APTA)

www.apta.org   703–684–APTA (2782) or 800–999–2782

Professional association for physical therapists. Multiple resources for professionals.

American Speech and Hearing Association (ASHA)

www.asha.org   Members: 800–498–2071; Nonmembers: 800–638–8255

Professional association for speech-language pathologists and audiologists. Multiple resources for professionals.

American Occupational Therapy Association (AOTA)

www.aota.org   301–652–2682

Professional association for occupational therapists. Multiple resources for professionals.

Association of University Centers on Disabilities (AUCD)

www.aucd.org   301–588–8252

A network of centers on disabilities for research, training, and service. A directory of the centers throughout the country is available.

Beach Center on Disability

www.beachcenter.org   785-864-7600

At the University of Kansas and part of Kansas' University Center on Disability, provides many resources on young children with disabilities and their families, for families and professionals.

Center for the Advanced Study of Excellence (CASE) in Early Childhood and Family Support

www.fippcase.org

A part of the Family, Infant, Preschool Program (FIPP), this Center provides evidence-based practices to support professionals in partnering with families. Also check out the related Coaching in Early Childhood Web site at www.coachinginearlychildhood.org/.

Center for Social Emotional Foundations for Early Learning (CSEFEL)

www.vanderbilt.edu/csefel/   1-866-433-1966

Federally funded center providing resources for families and professionals around promoting positive social-emotional development and positive behaviors in young children.

Division for Early Childhood of the Council for Exceptional Children (DEC)

www.dec-sped.org   406-543-0872

Professional association for those who work with or on behalf of young children with developmental delays or disabilities. Multiple resources for professionals.

Early Intervention Family Alliance

www.eifamilyalliance.org

A group committed to making sure that families actively participate in early intervention at the national, state, and local levels. Created and led by family leaders.

Family Village

www.familyvillage.wisc.edu

At the University of Wisconsin and sponsored by Wisconsin's University Center on Disability, provides information and resources for families and professionals specific to disability. Has many links to various Web sites that might be of interest to families and professionals.

Family Voices

www.familyvoices.org   505-872-4774 or Toll Free: 888-835-5669

A national network providing families with information and other supports to ensure family-centered care for all families with children with special health care needs and/or disabilities.

Frank Porter Graham Child Development Institute

www.fpg.unc.edu/   919-966-2622

At the University of North Carolina at Chapel Hill, has multiple research, training, and policy projects, centered on all children birth to 8 years and their families. Many projects focus specifically on young children with or at risk for developmental delay or disability.

Institute for Family Centered Care

www.familycenteredcare.org/   301-652-0281

Multiple resources for families and professionals to encourage family-centered services.

National Association for the Education of Young Children (NAEYC)

www.naeyc.org   202–232–8777

Professional organization for those who work with or on behalf of young children. Multiple resources for professionals.

National Dissemination Center for Children with Disabilities (NICHYC)

www.nichcy.org   800–695–0285

Provides a wide array of information related to children with disabilities for families, professionals, and the general public.

National Early Childhood Technical Assistance Center (NECTAC)

www.nectac.org   919–962–2001

Part of the Frank Porter Graham Child Development Institute, federally funded to support early intervention and preschool systems. Has multiple resources organized according to various topics (see Topics Pages), including current IDEA legislation and regulations. Provides conference presentations, publications, and Web-based resources. Provides a current list of Part C early intervention coordinators for each state and jurisdiction at www.nectac.org/contact/ptccoord.asp/. Has a searchable database of projects funded through the Office of Special Education Programs related to young children at www.nectac.org/search/projfinder.asp.

PACER Center

www.pacer.org   Minnesota: 800–537–2237, 952–838–9000; USA: 888–248–0822

Parent training and information (PTI) center providing resources, services, and materials for families with children with disabilities. National technical assistance center to all state PTIs, in partnership with regional technical assistance centers. Has a directory of all PTIs in the country.

Zero to Three

www.zerotothree.org   202–638–1144

Organization that provides various Web-based resources, publications, and videos on the development of infants and young children for families and professionals. Some sites require log in, but registration is free.

Appendix E

BIBLIOGRAPHY FOR FAMILIES

This appendix provides a list of written resources related to early intervention designed for families. Certainly early intervention professionals can choose to use them as well. Note: This list does not include the resources available through the Web sites listed in Appendix D.

Books

Jepson, E., & Thomas, J. (1999). *Essential allies, families as advisors.* Bethesda, MD: Institute for Family-Centered Care.

Klein, S., & Schive, K. (Eds.). (2001). *You will dream new dreams: Inspiring personal stories by parents of children with disabilities.* New York: Kensington Books.

Magazines

Exceptional Parent Magazine from EP Global Communications Inc. http://www.eparent.com

Publishers (books for families with children with disabilities)

Woodbine House (http://www.woodbinehouse.com/)
Special Needs Project (http://www.specialneeds.com/about.asp)

AppendixF

BIBLIOGRAPHY FOR PROFESSIONALS

This appendix provides a list of books and selected journals related to early inter-vention practices designed for early intervention professionals. Certainly families can choose to use them as well. Note: This list does not include books, journals, and other resources available through the professional associations and other Web sites listed in Appendix D.

Books

Bagnato, S. (2007). *Authentic assessment for early childhood intervention.* New York: Guilford.

Chen, D., Klein, M. D., Holloway, E., Myck-Wayne, J., Salcedo, P., & Snell, R. (2008). *Early intervention in action: Working across disciplines to support infants, young children, and their families* (CD-ROM). Baltimore: Brookes.

Guralnick, M. (2005). *The developmental systems approach to early intervention.* Baltimore: Brookes.

Hanft, B., Rush, D., & Shelden, M. (2004). *Coaching families and colleagues in early childhood.* Baltimore: Brookes.

Hanson, M., & Lynch, E. (2003). *Understanding families: Approaches to diversity, disability, and risk.* Baltimore: Brookes.

Howard, V., Williams, B., & Lepper, C. (2005). *Very young children with special needs: A formative approach for today's children.* New York: Pearson/Merrill Prentice Hall.

Klass, C. (2008). *The home visitor's guidebook: Promoting optimal parent and child development.* Baltimore: Brookes.

Rous, B., & Hallam, R. (2006). *Tools for transition in early childhood: A step-by-step guide for agencies, teachers, and families.* Baltimore: Brookes.

Snow, C., & Van Hemel, S. (2008). *Early childhood assessment: Why, what, and how?* Washington, DC: National Academy Press.

Turnbull, A., Turnbull, R., Erwin, E., & Soodak, L. (2006). *Families, professionals, and exceptionality: Positive outcomes through partnership and trust.* New York: Pearson/Merrill Prentice-Hall.

Journals

Early Childhood Services: An Interdisciplinary Journal of Effectiveness. Plural Publishing, Inc. (www.pluralpublishing.com/journals_ECS.htm)

Infants and Young Children. Lippincott, Williams and Wilkins (www.iycjournal.com)

Topics in Early Childhood Special Education. Hammill Institute on Disabilities (http://tec.sagepub.com/)

NOTES

Introduction

1. Bruder & Dunst, 2005
2. Guralnick, 1997
3. Sandall, Hemmeter, Smith, & McLean, 2005
4. IDEA, 2004
5. Dunst, 2000

Chapter 1

1. IDEA, 2004
2. Shackelford, 2006
3. IDEA, 2004, Sec. 632(5)(A)(ii)
4. Shackelford, 2006
5. IDEA, 2004
6. Guralnick, 2001a
7. Trivette & Dunst, 2005
8. Dunst, 2000
9. Wolery, 2000
10. Guralnick, 2001b
11. McWilliam, 2000

Chapter 2

1. Dunst, Trivette, Humphries, Raab, & Roper, 2001
2. Dunst, Hamby, Trivette, Raab, & Bruder, 2000
3. Keilty & Galvin, 2006; Kellegrew, 2000
4. Bronfenbrenner, 1993; Copple & Bredekamp, 2009
5. McWilliam, 2000
6. Ibid.
7. Sainato & Morrison, 2001
8. Ibid.; Sandall, Hemmeter, Smith, & McLean, 2005
9. McWilliam, 2000
10. Dunst, Bruder, Trivette, Raab, & McLean, 2001; Dunst, Trivette, Humphries, Raab, & Roper, 2001
11. Casey & McWilliam, 2007
12. McWilliam & Bailey, 1995
13. Bronfenbrenner, 1993; Bronfenbrenner, 1999; Copple & Bredekamp, 2009

14. Emde & Robinson, 2000
15. Keilty & Freund, 2004
16. Barrett, Morgan, & Maslin-Cole, 1993
17. Keilty & Freund, 2004
18. Busch-Rossnagel, 1997
19. Dunst, Bruder, Trivette, Raab, & McLean, 2001; Dunst, Trivette, Humphries, Raab, & Roper, 2001
20. Thomas & Chess, 1977
21. Dodici, Draper, & Peterson, 2003; Kelly & Barnard, 2000; Kim & Mahoney, 2004; National Research Council, 2000; Trivette, 2003
22. Kelly & Barnard, 2000
23. Ibid.
24. Chen, Klein, & Haney, 2007; Kelly, Zuckerman, & Rosenblatt, 2008
25. Carlson & Harwood, 1999/2000
26. National Research Council, 2000
27. Copple & Bredekamp, 2009
28. Wolery, 2004
29. Campbell, 2004
30. Ibid.
31. Vygotsky, 1978
32. National Research Council, 2000
33. Meléndez, 2005
34. National Research Council, 2000, p. 121
35. IDEA, 2004, Sec. 632(4)(G)
36. Ibid., Sec. 635(a)(16)(B)
37. Dunst, Hamby, Trivette, Raab, & Bruder, 2000, p. 161
38. IDEA, 2004, Sec. 635 (a)(3), Sec. 636(a)(1)
39. Hebbeler & Barton, 2007, p. 8
40. National Association for the Education of Young Children, 2002

Chapter 3

1. Guralnick, 2001a
2. Ibid.
3. Ibid.; Dunst, 2000
4. Dunst, 2000; Trivette & Dunst, 2005

5. Dunst, 1999; Dunst, 2000
6. Dunst, 2000
7. Trivette & Dunst, 2005, p. 107
8. Turnbull, Turnbull, Erwin, & Soodak, 2006
9. Bernheimer & Weisner, 2007
10. Ibid.
11. Ibid.; Gallimore, Weisner, Kaufman, &
    Bernheimer, 1989
12. Bernheimer & Weisner, 2007; Gallimore,
    Weisner, Kaufman, & Bernheimer, 1989
13. Bailey, Bruder, Hebbeler, Carta, Defosset,
    Greenwood, et al., 2006; Guralnick, 2001a
14. Turnbull, Turnbull, Erwin, & Soodak, 2006
15. Trivette & Dunst, 2005
16. Bailey, 2001; McConnell, 2001; Turnbull,
    Summers, Turnbull, Brotherson, Winton,
    Roberts, et al., 2007
17. Hebbeler & Barton, 2007
18. Banks, Milagros Santos, & Roof, 2003
19. Ibid.
20. Dunst & Trivette, 1996; Trivette & Dunst,
    2005
21. Roberts, Rule, & Innocenti, 1998
22. Schwartz & Rodriguez, 2001
23. Guralnick, 2001a; Turnbull, Turnbull, Erwin,
    & Soodak, 2006
24. Bailey, Bruder, Hebbeler, Carta, Defosset,
    Greenwood, et al., 2006; Guralnick, 2001a;
    McWilliam & Scott, 2001
25. McCormick, Stricklin, Nowak, & Rous, 2008
26. Dunst, 2000
27. Dunst & Dempsey, 2007
28. Dunst, 2000; Trivette & Dunst, 2005
29. Turnbull, Turnbull, Erwin, & Soodak, 2006,
    p. 141
30. Bailey, 2001; Trivette, Dunst, & Hamby, 1996
31. Dunst, 2000; Dunst & Trivette, 1996; Trivette &
    Dunst, 2005; Trivette, Dunst, & Hamby, 1996
32. Dunst, 2000
33. Turnbull, Summers, Turnbull, Brotherson,
    Winton, Roberts, et al., 2007
34. Banks, Milagros Santos, & Roof, 2003
35. Wyngaarden Krauss, 2000
36. IDEA, 2004, Sec. 636(a)(2)
37. Federal Regulations for Early Intervention
    Program for Infants and Toddlers with
    Disabilities, 1999
38. Hebbeler & Barton, 2007, p. 9
39. Sandall, Hemmeter, Smith, & McLean, 2005
40. Trivette & Dunst, 2005, p.116

Chapter 4

1. Greenspan & Meisels, 1996, p. 11

2. Neisworth & Bagnato, 2004
3. Brink, 2002; Squires, Potter, Bricker, Lamorey,
   1998
4. Neisworth & Bagnato, 2005, p. 48
5. McLean, 2004
6. Mott & Dunst, 2006
7. McLean, 2004
8. Ibid.
9. Vig & Kaminer, 2003
10. McWilliam, 2003
11. Dunst, Bruder, Trivette, Raab, & McLean, 2001;
    McWilliam, 2003; TACTICS Project, 2000
12. Bronfenbrenner, 1977, p. 513
13. Bagnato, 2005
14. Ibid.
15. Bagnato, 2007; Grisham-Brown, Hallam,
    & Pretti-Frontczak, 2008; Neisworth &
    Bagnato, 2004
16. Copple & Bredekamp, 2009; Sandall,
    Hemmeter, Smith, & McLean, 2005
17. Campbell, 2004; Stremel & Campbell, 2007
18. Meisels & Atkins-Burnett, 2000
19. Wilson, Mott, Batman, 2004
20. Jung & Grisham-Brown, 2006; Wolery, 2005
21. Keilty & Galvin, 2006
22. Woods & McCormick, 2002
23. Campbell, 2004
24. Woods & McCormick, 2002
25. Neisworth & Bagnato, 2005
26. Losardo & Notari-Syverson, 2001
27. Lynch, 2007
28. Meisels & Atkins-Burnett, 2000
29. Suen, Logan, Neisworth, & Bagnato, 1995
30. Sandall, Hemmeter, Smith, & McLean,
    2005
31. Federal Regulations for Early Intervention
    Program for Infants and Toddlers with
    Disabilities, 1999
32. Ibid., Sec. 303.322(b)(2)(i)
33. IDEA, 2004
34. Federal Regulations for Early Intervention
    Program for Infants and Toddlers with
    Disabilities, 1999
35. Shackelford, 2002
36. Copple & Bredekamp, 2009, p. 22
37. Hebbeler & Barton, 2007
38. McLean, 2004
39. Early Childhood Outcomes Center, 2006

Chapter 5

1. Jung & McWilliam, 2005
2. Ibid.
3. McWilliam, R.A., 1996; Rapport, McWilliam,

& Smith, 2004; Sandall, Hemmeter, Smith, & McLean, 2005
4. Rosenkoetter & Squires, 2000
5. Jung & Grisham-Brown, 2006
6. Sandall, Hemmeter, Smith, & McLean, 2005
7. McWilliam, R.A., 1996
8. Jung, 2007; Sandall, Hemmeter, Smith, & McLean, 2005
9. Weintraub Moore & Wilcox, 2006
10. IDEA, 2004, Sec. 632(4)(G)
11. Dunst, Hamby, Trivette, Raab, & Bruder, 2000
12. Wolery, 2005
13. McWilliam, 2000
14. Ibid.
15. Jung, 2003; McWilliam, R.A., 1996
16. Jung, 2003
17. Dunst, Trivette, Humphries, Raab, & Roper, 2001; McWilliam, 2000
18. Jung, 2003
19. Ibid.
20. Affleck, Tennen, Rowe, Roscher, & Walker, 1989
21. McWilliam, P.J., 1996
22. Rapport, McWilliam, & Smith, 2004
23. Ibid.; Bruder, 1996; Jung, 2005
24. Jung, 2005
25. Ibid.
26. Bruder, 1996
27. Ibid.; Rapport, McWilliam, & Smith, 2004
28. Bruder, 1996
29. Ibid.; McWilliam, R.A., 1996
30. Bruder, 1996; McWilliam, R.A., 1996; Rapport, McWilliam, & Smith, 2004
31. Rapport, McWilliam, & Smith, 2004
32. Sandall, Hemmeter, Smith, & McLean, 2005
33. McWilliam, R.A., 1996; Rapport, McWilliam, & Smith, 2004
34. Kaczmarek, Pennington, & Goldstein, 2000; Rapport, McWilliam, & Smith, 2004
35. Dunst, 1999
36. Bruder, 1996
37. Ibid.; Sandall, Hemmeter, Smith, & McLean, 2005
38. McWilliam, R.A., 1996; Rapport, McWilliam, & Smith, 2004
39. McWilliam, P.J., 1996
40. Sandall, Hemmeter, Smith, & McLean, 2005
41. Bruder, 1996
42. Sandall, Hemmeter, Smith, & McLean, 2005
43. McWilliam, P.J., 1996
44. Ibid.
45. Sandall, Hemmeter, Smith, & McLean, 2005
46. Jung & Grisham-Brown, 2006

47. Winton, 1996
48. Ohtake, Santos, & Fowler, 2000
49. Jung & McWilliam, 2005
50. IDEA, 2004
51. Federal Regulations for Early Intervention Program for Infants and Toddlers with Disabilities, 1999
52. Ibid., §303.323 (a)
53. IDEA, 2004, Sec. 636(d)(3)
54. Ibid., Sec. 635(a)(2)
55. Ibid., Sec. 636(d)(4)
56. Sandall, Hemmeter, Smith, & McLean, 2005
57. Council on Children with Disabilities, 2007

Chapter 6

1. McWilliam, 2000
2. Campbell & Sawyer, 2007; McBride & Peterson, 1997; Peterson, Luze, Eshbaugh, Jeon, & Ross Kantz, 2007
3. Bruder, 2000; Shelden & Rush, 2001; Stremel & Campbell, 2007
4. Keilty, 2008
5. McWilliam, 2000
6. Ibid.
7. Keilty, 2008
8. McWilliam, 2000
9. Keilty, 2008, p. 36
10. Bernheimer & Keogh, 1995, p. 424
11. McWilliam, 2000
12. Keilty, 2008
13. Ibid.
14. Ibid.
15. Kaiser & Hancock, 2003; Mobayed, Collins, Strangis, Schuster, & Hemmeter, 2000; Woods, Kashinath, & Goldstein, 2004
16. Keilty, 2008
17. Ibid.
18. Ibid.
19. Keilty & Galvin, 2006
20. Luze & Peterson, 2004
21. Ibid.; Halle, 1998
22. Sandall, Hemmeter, Smith, & McLean, 2005, p. 138

Chapter 7

1. Dunst, 2001
2. Wolery, 2005
3. Dunst, Hamby, Trivette, Raab, & Bruder, 2000
4. Dunst, Herter, Sheilds, & Bennis, 2001
5. Dunst, 2001
6. Campbell, 2004
7. Ibid.

8. Bruder, 2001
9. Hanft, Rush, & Shelden, 2004
10. Sandall, Hemmeter, Smith, & McLean, 2005
11. Hanft, Rush, & Shelden, 2004
12. Dunst, 2001; Sandall, Hemmeter, Smith, & McLean, 2005
13. Sandall, Hemmeter, Smith, & McLean, 2005, p. 80

Chapter 8

1. Dunst & Bruder, 2002
2. Ibid.
3. Roberts, Rule, & Innocenti, 1998, p. 51
4. Allen, 2007
5. Bruder, Harbin, Whitbread, Conn-Powers, Roberts, Dunst, et al., 2005, p. 186
6. Ibid.
7. Ibid.
8. Dunst & Bruder, 2006
9. Ibid.
10. Ibid.
11. IDEA, 2004, Sec. 636(d)(7)
12. Federal Regulations for Early Intervention Program for Infants and Toddlers with Disabilities, 1999, §303.23(a)(1)
13. Federal Regulations for Early Intervention Program for Infants and Toddlers with Disabilities, 1999, §303.23(b)

Chapter 9

1. National Research Council, 2000
2. Ibid.
3. Ibid., p. 371
4. Campbell, 2004; Stremel & Campbell, 2007
5. Dunlap, Ester, Langhans, & Fox, 2006
6. Wolery, 2004
7. Busch-Rossnagel, 1997
8. Keilty & Freund, 2004
9. Hauser-Cram, 1998
10. McCall, 1995
11. Keilty & Freund, 2004
12. Field, Martin, Miller, Ward, & Wehmeyer, 1998
13. See, e.g., Karvonen, Test, Wood, Browder, & Algozzine, 2004; Martin, Mithaug, Cox, Peterson, Van Dycke, & Cash, 2003; Palmer, Wehmeyer, Gipson, & Agran, 2004

14. Brotherson, Cook, Erwin, & Weigel, 2008; Cho & Palmer, 2008; Mulhearn Blasco, Falco, & Munson, 2006; Shogren & Turnbull, 2006
15. Brotherson, Cook, Erwin, & Weigel, 2008; Cho & Palmer, 2008; Mulhearn Blasco, Falco, & Munson, 2006
16. Brotherson, Cook, Erwin, & Weigel, 2008
17. Ibid.; Shogren & Turnbull, 2006
18. Guralnick, 2001a
19. Turnbull, Turnbull, Erwin, & Soodak, 2006
20. Connelly, 2007; Fox, Dunlap, & Cushing, 2002; Hanson, Beckman, Horn, Marquart, Sandall, Greig, et al., 2000
21. National Research Council, 2000
22. IDEA, 2004
23. Fox, Dunlap, & Cushing, 2002; Hanson, Beckman, Horn, Marquart, Sandall, Greig, et al., 2000; Lovett & Haring, 2003; Rous, Myers, & Stricklin, 2007
24. Rous & Hallam, 2006
25. Connelly, 2007; Rous & Hallam, 2006; Rous, Myers, & Stricklin, 2007
26. Lovett & Haring, 2003
27. Lovett & Haring, 2003; Rous, Myers, & Stricklin, 2007
28. Sainato & Morrison, 2001
29. Rous & Hallam, 2006; Rous, Hallam, Harbin, McCormick, & Jung, 2007; Rous, Myers, & Stricklin, 2007
30. Sainato & Morrison, 2001
31. Harbin, Rous, Peeler, Schuster, & McCormick, 2007
32. IDEA, 2004, Sec. 612(a)(5)(A)
33. Guralnick, 2001b
34. Sandall, Hemmeter, Smith, & McLean, 2005; Wolery, 2000
35. Federal Regulations for Early Intervention Program for Infants and Toddlers with Disabilities, 1999; IDEA, 2004
36. Federal Regulations for Early Intervention Program for Infants and Toddlers with Disabilities, 1999, §303.344(h)(2)(i-ii)

Chapter 10

1. IDEA, 2004

REFERENCES

Affleck, G., Tennen, H., Rowe, J., Roscher, B., & Walker, L. (1989). Effects of formal support on mothers' adaptation to the hospital-to-home transition of high-risk infants: The benefits and costs of helping. *Child Development, 60,* 488–501.

Allen, S. (2007). Parents' perspectives: An evaluation of case management interventions in home visiting programs for young children. *Children & Schools, 29,* 75–85.

Bagnato, S. (2005). The authentic alternative for assessment in early intervention: An emerging evidence-based practice. *Journal of Early Intervention, 28,* 17–22.

Bagnato, S. (2007). *Authentic Assessment for Early Childhood Intervention: Best Practices.* New York: Guilford Press, Inc.

Bailey, D. (2001). Evaluating parent involvement and family support in early intervention and preschool programs. *Journal of Early Intervention, 24,* 1–14.

Bailey, D., Bruder, M., Hebbeler, K., Carta, J., Defosset, M., Greenwood, C., Kahn, L., Mallik, S., Markowitz, J., Spiker, D., Walker, D., & Barton L. (2006). Recommended outcomes for families of young children with disabilities. *Journal of Early Intervention, 28,* 227–251.

Banks, R., Milagros Santos, R., & Roof, V. (2003). Discovering family concerns, priorities, and resources: Sensitive family information gathering. *Young Exceptional Children,* 6(2) 11–19.

Barrett, K., Morgan, G., & Maslin-Cole, C. (1993). Three studies on the development of mastery motivation in infancy and toddlerhood. In D. Messer (Ed.), *Mastery motivation in early childhood: Development, measurement, and social processes* (pp. 168–188). London: Routledge.

Bernheimer, L., & Keogh, B. (1995). Weaving interventions into the fabric of everyday life: An approach to family assessment. *Topics in Early Childhood Special Education, 15,* 415–433.

Bernheimer, L., & Weisner, T. (2007). "Let me just tell you what I do all day . . . ": The family story at the center of intervention research and practice. *Infants and Young Children, 20,* 192–201.

Brink, M.B. (2002). Involving parents in early childhood assessment: Perspectives from an early intervention instructor. *Early Childhood Education Journal, 29,* 251–257.

Bronfenbrenner, U. (1977). Toward an experimental ecology of human development. *American Psychologist, 32,* 513–531.

Bronfenbrenner, U. (1993). The ecology of cognitive development: Research models and fugitive findings. In R.H. Wozniak & K.W. Fischer (Eds.), *Development in context: Acting and thinking in specific environments* (pp. 3–44). Hillsdale, NJ: Lawrence Erlbaum.

Bronfenbrenner, U. (1999). Environments in developmental perspective: Theoretical and operational models. In S.L. Friedman & T.D. Wachs (Eds.), *Emerging methods and concepts* (pp. 3–28). Washington, DC: American Psychological Association.

Brotherson, M.J., Cook, C., Erwin, E., & Weigel, C. (2008). Understanding self-determination and families of young children with disabilities in home environments. *Journal of Early Intervention, 31,* 22–43.

Bruder, M. (1996) Interdisciplinary collaboration in service delivery. In R.A. McWilliam, (Ed.), *Rethinking pull-out services in early intervention: A professional resource* (pp. 27–48). Baltimore, MD: Brookes.

Bruder, M.B. (2000). Family centered early intervention: Clarifying our values for the new millennium. *Topics in Early Childhood Special Education, 20,* 105–115.

Bruder, M.B. (2001) Inclusion of infants and toddlers: Outcomes and ecology. In M.J. Guralnick (Ed.), *Early childhood inclusion: Focus on change* (pp. 203–228). Baltimore: Brookes.

Bruder, M.B., & Dunst, C. (2005). Personnel preparation in recommended early intervention practices: Degree of emphasis. *Topics in Early Childhood Special Education, 25,* 25–33.

Bruder, M.B., Harbin, G., Whitbread, K., Conn-Powers, M., Roberts, R., Dunst, C., Van Buren, M., Mazzarella, C., & Gabbard, G. (2005). Establishing outcomes for service coordination: A step toward evidence-based practice. *Topics in Early Childhood Special Education, 25,* 177–188.

Busch-Rossnagel, N. (1997). Mastery motivation in toddlers. *Infants and Young Children, 9,* 1–11.

Campbell, P. (2004). Participation-based services: Promoting children's participation in natural settings. *Young Exceptional Children, 8,*(1) 20–29.

Campbell, P., & Sawyer, B. (2007). Supporting learning opportunities in natural settings through participation-based services. *Journal of Early Intervention, 29,* 287–305.

Carlson, V., & Harwood, R. (1999/2000). Understanding and negotiating cultural differences concerning early developmental competence: The six raisin solution. *Zero to Three, 19–24,*

Casey, A., & McWilliam, R. (2007). The STARE: The Scale for Teachers' Assessment of Routines Engagement. *Young Exceptional Children, 11*(1) 2–15.

Chen, D., Klein, M., & Haney, M. (2007). Promoting interactions with infants who have complex multiple disabilities: Development and field-testing of the PLAI curriculum. *Infants and Young Children, 20,* 149–162.

Cho, H., & Palmer, S. (2008). Fostering self-determination in infants and toddlers with visual impairments or blindness. *Young Exceptional Children, 11*(4) 26–34.

Connelly, A. (2007). Transitions of families from early intervention to preschool intervention for children with disabilities. *Young Exceptional Children, 10*(3) 10–16.

Copple, C., & Bredekamp, S. (Eds.). (2009). *Developmentally Appropriate Practice in Early Childhood Programs Serving Children from Birth through Age 8.* Washington, DC: NAEYC.

Council on Children with Disabilities. (2007). Role of the medical home in family-centered early intervention services. *Pediatrics, 120,* 1153–1158.

Dodici, B., Draper, D., & Peterson, C. (2003). Early parent–child interactions and early literacy development. *Topics in Early Childhood Special Education, 23,* 124–136.

Dunlap, G., Ester, T., Langhans, S., & Fox, L. (2006). Functional communication training with toddlers in home environments. *Journal of Early Intervention, 28,* 81–96.

Dunst, C. (1999). Placing parent education in conceptual and empirical context. *Topics in Early Childhood Special Education, 19,* 141–147.

Dunst, C. (2000). Revisiting "Rethinking Early Intervention." *Topics in Early Childhood Special Education, 20,* 95–104.

Dunst, C. (2001). Participation of young children with disabilities in community learning activities. In M.J. Guralnick (Ed.), *Early childhood inclusion: Focus on change* (pp. 307–333). Baltimore: Brookes.

Dunst, C., & Bruder, M.B. (2002). Valued outcomes of service coordination, early intervention, and natural environments. *Exceptional Children, 68* 361–375.

Dunst, C., & Bruder, M.B. (2006). Early intervention service coordination models and service coordinator practices. *Journal of Early Intervention, 28,* 155–165.

Dunst, C., Bruder, M.B., Trivette, C., Raab, M., & McLean, M. (2001). Natural learning opportunities for infants, toddlers, and preschoolers. *Young Exceptional Children,* 4(3) 18–25.

Dunst, C., & Dempsey, I. (2007). Family-professional partnerships and parenting competence, confidence, and enjoyment. *International Journal of Disability, Development and Education, 54,* 305–318.

Dunst, C., Hamby, D., Trivette, C., Raab, M., & Bruder, M.B. (2000). Everyday family and community life and children's naturally occurring learning opportunities. *Journal of Early Intervention, 23,* 151–164.

Dunst, C., Herter, S., Sheilds, H., & Bennis, L. (2001). Mapping community-based natural learning opportunities. *Young Exceptional Children,* 4(4) 16–25.

Dunst, C., & Trivette, C. (1996). Empowerment, effective helpgiving practices and family-centered care. *Pediatric Nursing, 22,* 334–343.

Dunst, C., Trivette, C., Humphries, T., Raab, M., & Roper, N. (2001). Contrasting approaches to natural learning environment interventions. *Infants and Young Children, 14,* 48–63.

Early Childhood Outcomes Center. (2006). *Overview of the child outcomes summary form.* Menlo Park, CA: SRI International.

Emde, R., & Robinson, J. (2000). Guiding principles for a theory of early intervention: A developmental-psychoanalytic perspective. In J.P. Shonkoff & S.J. Meisels (Eds.), *Handbook of early childhood intervention* (2nd ed., pp. 160–178). Cambridge, UK: Cambridge University Press.

Federal Regulations for Early Intervention Program for Infants and Toddlers with Disabilities, 34 CFR 303.1 (1999).

Field, S., Martin, J., Miller, R., Ward, M., & Wehmeyer, M. (1998). *Self-determination for persons with disabilities: A position statement of the division on career development and transition.* Retrieved December 26, 2008 from http://www.dcdt.org/publications/index.html#position.

Fox, L., Dunlap, G., & Cushing, L. (2002). Early intervention, positive behavior support, and transition to school. *Journal of Emotional and Behavioral Disorders, 10,* 149–157.

Gallimore, R., Weisner, T., Kaufman, S., & Bernheimer, L. (1989). The social construction of ecocultural niches: Family accommodation of developmentally delayed children. *American Journal of Mental Deficiency, 94,* 216–230.

Greenspan, S. & Meisels, S. J. (1996). Toward a new vision for the developmental assessment of infants and young children. In S. Meisels & E. Fenichel (Eds.) *New visions for the developmental assessment of infants and young children* (pp. 11–26). Washington, DC: Zero to Three.

Grisham-Brown, J., Hallam, R., & Pretti-Frontczak, K. (2008). Preparing Head Start personnel to use a curriculum-based assessment: An innovative practice in the "age of accountability." *Journal of Early Intervention, 30,* 271–281.

Guralnick, M.J. (1997). Second generation research in the field of early intervention. In M.J. Guralnick (Ed.), *The effectiveness of early intervention* (pp. 3–20). Baltimore: Brookes.

Guralnick, M. (2001a). A developmental systems model for early intervention. *Infants and Young Children, 14,* 1–18.

Guralnick, M.J. (2001b). *Early childhood inclusion: Focus on change.* Baltimore: Brookes.

Halle, J. (1998). Fidelity: A crucial question in translating research into practice. *Journal of Early Intervention, 21,* 294–296.

Hanft, B., Rush, D., & Shelden, M. (2004). *Coaching families and colleagues in early childhood.* Baltimore: Brookes.

Hanson, M., Beckman, P., Horn, E., Marquart, J., Sandall, S., Greig, D., & Brennan, E. (2000). Entering preschool: Family and professional experiences in this transition process. *Journal of Early Intervention, 23,* 279–293.

Harbin, G., Rous, B., Peeler, N., Schuster, J., & McCormick, K. (2007, December). *Research brief: Desired family outcomes of the early childhood transition process.* Lexington: University of Kentucky, National Early Childhood Transition Center.

Hauser-Cram, P. (1998). I think I can, I think I can: Understanding and encouraging mastery motivation in young children. *Young Children, 53,* 67–71.

Hebbeler, K., & Barton, L. (2007). The need for data on child and family outcomes at the federal and state levels. In E. Horn, C. Peterson, and L. Fox (Eds.), *Young Exceptional Children monograph series no. 9: Linking curriculum to child and family outcomes* (pp. 1–15). Missoula, MT: Division for Early Childhood of the Council for Exceptional Children.

Individuals with Disabilities Education Improvement Act of 2004, 20 U.S.C. § 1400 et seq. (2004).

Jung, L.A. (2003). More IS better: Maximizing natural learning opportunities. *Young Exceptional Children, 6*(3) 21–26.

Jung, L.A. (2005). Can we all fit? Squeezing in better support with fewer people. *Young Exceptional Children, 8*(4) 19–27.

Jung, L.A. (2007). Writing Individualized Family Service Plan strategies that fit into the Routine. *Young Exceptional Children, 10*(3) 2–9.

Jung, L.A., & Grisham-Brown, J. (2006). Moving from assessment information to IFSPs: Guidelines for a family-centered process. *Young Exceptional Children, 9*(2) 2–11.

Jung, L.A., & McWilliam, R.A. (2005). Reliability and validity of scores on the IFSP rating scale. *Journal of Early Intervention, 27,* 125–136.

Kaczmarek, L., Pennington, R., & Goldstein, H. (2000). Transdisciplinary consultation: A center-based team functioning model. *Education and Treatment of Children, 23,*156–172.

Kaiser, A., & Hancock, T. (2003). Teaching parents new skills to support their young children's development. *Infants and Young Children, 16,* 9–21.

Karvonen, M., Test, D., Wood, W., Browder, D., & Algozzine, B. (2004). Putting self-determination into practice. *Exceptional Children, 71,* 23–41.

Keilty, B. (2008). Early intervention home visiting principles in practice: A reflective approach. *Young Exceptional Children, 11*(2) 29–40.

Keilty, B., & Freund, M. (2004). Mastery motivation: A framework for considering the "how" of learning in infants and toddlers. *Young Exceptional Children, 8*(1) 2–10.

Keilty, B., & Galvin, K. (2006). Physical and social adaptations families make to promote learning in everyday experiences. *Topics in Early Childhood Special Education, 26,* 219–233.

Kellegrew, D. (2000). Constructing daily routines: A qualitative examination of mothers with young children with disabilities. *The American Journal of Occupational Therapy, 54,* 252–259.

Kelly, J., & Barnard, K. (2000). Assessment of parent–child interaction: Implications for early intervention. In J.P. Shonkoff & S.J. Meisels (Eds.), *Handbook of early childhood intervention* (2nd ed., pp. 258–289). Cambridge, UK: Cambridge University Press.

Kelly, J., Zuckerman, T., & Rosenblatt, S. (2008). Promoting first relationships: A relationship-focused early intervention approach. *Infants and Young Children, 21,* 285–295.

Kim, J., & Mahoney, G. (2004). The effects of mother's style of interaction on children's engagement: Implications for using responsive interventions with parents. *Topics in Early Childhood Special Education, 24,* 31–38.

Losardo, A., & Notari-Syverson, A. (2001). *Alternative approaches to assessing young children.* Baltimore: Brookes.

Lovett, D., & Haring, K. (2003). Family perceptions of transitions in early intervention. *Education and Training in Developmental Disabilities, 38,* 370–377.

Luze, G., & Peterson, C. (2004). Improving outcomes for young children by assessing intervention integrity and monitoring progress: "Am I doing it right and is it working?" *Young Exceptional Children, 7*(2) 20–29.

Lynch, E. (2007). Authentic assessment in the inclusive classroom: Using portfolios to document change and modify curriculum. In E. Horn, C. Peterson, and L. Fox (Eds.), *Young Exceptional Children monograph series no. 9: Linking curriculum to child and family outcomes* (pp. 55–70). Missoula, MT: Division for Early Childhood of the Council for Exceptional Children.

Martin, J., Mithaug, D., Cox, P., Peterson, L., Van Dycke, J., & Cash, M. (2003). Increasing self-determination: Teaching students to plan, work, evaluate, and adjust. *Exceptional Children, 69,* 431–447.

McBride, S., & Peterson, C. (1997). Home-based early intervention with families of children with disabilities: Who is doing what? *Topics in Early Childhood Special Education, 17,* 209–233.

McCall, R. (1995). On definitions and measures of mastery motivation, In R.H. MacTurk & G.A. Morgan (Eds.), *Mastery motivation: Origins, conceptualizations, and applications* (pp. 273–292). Norwood, NJ: Ablex.

McConnell, S. (2001). Parent involvement and family support: Where do we want to go, and how will we know we are headed there? *Journal of Early Intervention, 24,* 15–18.

McCormick, K., Stricklin, S., Nowak, T., & Rous, B. (2008). Using eco-mapping to understand family strengths and resources. *Young Exceptional Children, 11*(2) 17–28.

McLean, M. (2004). Assessment and its importance in early intervention/early childhood special education. In M. McLean, M. Wolery, & D. Bailey (Eds.), *Assessing infants and preschoolers with special needs* (3rd ed., pp. 1–21). Englewood Cliffs, NJ: Merrill/Prentice Hall.

McWilliam, P.J. (1996). Collaborative consultation across seven disciplines: Challenges and solutions. In R.A. McWilliam, (Ed.), *Rethinking pull-out services in early intervention: A professional resource* (pp. 315–340). Baltimore: Brookes.

McWilliam, R.A. (1996). Implications for the future of integrating specialized services. In
   R. McWilliam, (Ed.), *Rethinking pull-out services in early intervention: A professional
   resource* (pp. 343–371). Baltimore: Brookes.
McWilliam, R.A. (2000). It's only natural . . . to have early intervention in the
   environments where it's needed. In S. Sandall and M. Ostrosky (Eds.), *Young
   Exceptional Children monograph series no. 2: Natural environments and inclusion* (pp.
   17–26). Longmont, CO: Sopris West.
McWilliam, R.A. (2003). RBI report form. Center for Child Development, Vanderbilt
   University Medical Center, Nashville, TN.
McWilliam, R.A., & Bailey, D. (1995). Effects of classroom social structure and disability
   on engagement. *Topics in Early Childhood Special Education, 15*, 123–148.
McWilliam, R.A., & Scott, S. (2001). A support approach to early intervention: A three-
   part framework. *Infants and Young Children, 13*, 55–66.
Meisels, S.J., & Atkins-Burnett, S. (2000). The elements of early childhood assessment. In
   J.P. Shonkoff & S.J. Meisels (Eds.), *Handbook of early childhood intervention* (2nd ed.,
   pp. 231–257). Cambridge, UK: Cambridge University Press.
Meléndez, R.L. (2005). Parental beliefs and practices around early self-regulation: The
   impact of culture and immigration. *Infants and Young Children, 18*, 136–146.
Mobayed, K., Collins, B., Strangis, D., Schuster, J., & Hemmeter, M. (2000). Teaching
   parents to employ mand-model procedures to teach their children requesting.
   Journal of Early Intervention, 23, 165–179.
Mott, D., & Dunst, C. (2006). Use of presumptive eligibility for enrolling children in Part
   C early intervention. *Journal of Early Intervention, 29*, 22–31.
Mulhearn Blasco, P., Falco, R., & Munson, L. (2006). Project SELF: Preparing
   professionals to facilitate self-determination. *Journal of Early Intervention, 29*, 63–79.
National Association for the Education of Young Children. (2002). *Early Learning
   Standards: Creating the Conditions for Success*. Washington, DC: Author.
National Research Council, Committee on Integrating the Science of Early Childhood
   Development. (2000). *From neurons to neighborhoods: The science of early childhood
   development*. Washington, DC: National Academy Press.
Neisworth, J., & Bagnato, S. (2004). The mismeasure of young children: The authentic
   assessment alternative. *Infants and Young Children, 17*, 198–212.
Neisworth, J., & Bagnato, S. (2005). DEC recommended practices: Assessment
   (Introduction). In S. Sandall, M.L. Hemmeter, B.J. Smith, & M.E. McLean, *DEC
   recommended practices: A comprehensive guide for practical application in early
   intervention/early childhood special education* (pp. 45–50). Missoula, MT: Division for
   Early Childhood.
Ohtake, Y., Santos, R., & Fowler, S. (2000). It's a three-way conversation: Families, service
   providers, and interpreters working together. *Young Exceptional Children, 4*(1) 12–18.
Palmer, S., Wehmeyer, M., Gipson, K., & Agran, M. (2004). Promoting access to the
   general curriculum by teaching self-determination skills. *Exceptional Children, 70*,
   427–439.
Peterson, C., Luze, G., Eshbaugh, E., Jeon, H-J., & Ross Kantz, K. (2007). Enhancing
   parent–child interactions through home visiting: Promising practice or unfulfilled
   promise. *Journal of Early Intervention, 29*, 119–140.
Rapport, M.J., McWilliam, R.A., & Smith, B. (2004). Practices across disciplines in early
   intervention: The research base. *Infants and Young Children, 17*, 32–33.

Roberts, R., Rule, S., & Innocenti, M. (1998). *Strengthening the family–professional partnership in services for young children*. Baltimore: Brookes.

Rosenkoetter, S., & Squires, S. (2000). Writing outcomes that make a difference for children and families. *Young Exceptional Children, 4*(1) 2–8.

Rous, B., & Hallam, R. (2006). *Tools for transition in early childhood: A step-by-step guide for agencies, teachers, & families*. Baltimore: Brookes.

Rous, B., Hallam, R., Harbin, G., McCormick, K., & Jung, L. (2007). The transition process for young children with disabilities: A conceptual framework. *Infants and Young Children, 20*, 135–148.

Rous, B., Myers, C.T. & Stricklin, S. (2007). Strategies for supporting transitions for young children with special needs. *Journal of Early Intervention 30*(1), 1–18.

Sainato, D., & Morrison , R. (2001). Transition to inclusive environments for young children with disabilities: Toward a seamless system of service delivery. In M.J. Guralnick (Ed.), *Early childhood inclusion: Focus on change* (pp. 293–306). Baltimore: Brookes.

Sandall, S., Hemmeter, M.L., Smith, B., & McLean, M. (2005). *DEC Recommended practices: A comprehensive guide for practical application in early intervention/early childhood special education*. Missoula, MT: Division for Early Childhood.

Schwartz, I., & Rodriguez, P. (2001). A few issues to consider: The who, what, and where of family support. *Journal of Early Intervention, 24*, 19–21.

Shackelford, J. (2002). *Informed clinical opinion* (NECTAC Notes No. 10). Chapel Hill: The University of North Carolina, FPG Child Development Institute, National Early Childhood Technical Assistance Center.

Shackelford, J. (2006). *State and jurisdictional eligibility definitions for infants and toddlers with disabilities under IDEA* (NECTAC Notes No. 21). Chapel Hill: The University of North Carolina, FPG Child Development Institute, National Early Childhood Technical Assistance Center.

Shelden, M., & Rush, D. (2001). The ten myths about providing early intervention services in natural environments. *Infants and Young Children, 14*, 1–3.

Shogren, K. A. & Turnbull, A. (2006). Promoting self-determination in young children with disabilities: The critical role of families. *Infants and Young Children, 19*, 338–352.

Squires, J., Potter, L., Bricker, D., & Lamorey, S. (1998). Parent-completed developmental questionnaires: Effectiveness with low and middle income parents. *Early Childhood Research Quarterly, 13*, 345–354.

Stremel, K., & Campbell, P. (2007). Implementation of early intervention within natural environments. *Early Childhood Services: An Interdisciplinary Journal of Effectiveness, 1*, 83–105.

Suen, H., Logan, C.R., Neisworth, J., & Bagnato, S. (1995). Parent-professional congruence: Is it necessary? *Journal of Early Intervention, 19*, 243–252.

TACTICS Project. (2000). Identifying family activities and routines: Conversation starters. Florida State University, Tallahassee, FL.

Thomas, A., & Chess, S. (1977). *Temperament and development*. New York: Brunner/Mazel.

Trivette, C. (2003, June). Influence of caregiver responsiveness on the development of young children with or at risk for developmental disabilities. *Bridges: Practice based research syntheses, 1*(3). Asheville, NC: Research and Training Center on Early Childhood Development, Puckett Center.

Trivette, C., & Dunst, C. (2005). DEC recommended practices: Family-based practices (Introduction). In S. Sandall, M.L. Hemmeter, B.J. Smith, & M.E. McLean, *DEC recommended practices: A comprehensive guide for practical application in early intervention/early childhood special education* (pp. 107–112). Missoula, MT: Division for Early Childhood.

Trivette, C., Dunst, C., & Hamby, D. (1996). Factors associated with perceived control appraisals in a family-centered early intervention program. *Journal of Early Intervention, 20,* 165–178.

Turnbull, A., Summers, J., Turnbull, R., Brotherson, M., Winton, P., Roberts, R., Snyder, P., McWilliam, R.A., Chandler, L., Schrandt, S., Stowe, M., Bruder, M. B., DiVenere, N., Epley, P., Hornback, M., Huff, B., Miksch, P., Mitchell, L., Sharp, L., & Stroup-Rentier, V. (2007). Family supports and services in early intervention: A bold vision. *Journal of Early Intervention, 29,* 187–206.

Turnbull, A., Turnbull, R., Erwin, E., & Soodak, L. (2006). *Families, professionals, and exceptionality: Positive outcomes through partnerships and trust* (5th ed.). Upper Saddle River, NJ: Pearson Merrill Prentice-Hall.

Vig, S., & Kaminer, R. (2003). Comprehensive interdisciplinary evaluation as intervention for young children. *Infants and Young Children, 16*(4), 342–353.

Vygotsky, L. S. (1978). *Mind in society: The development of higher psychological processes.* Cambridge, MA: Harvard University Press.

Weintraub Moore, H., & Wilcox, M.J. (2006). Characteristics of early intervention practitioners and their confidence in the use of assistive technology. *Topics in Early Childhood Special Education, 26,* 15–23.

Wilson, L.L., Mott, D.W., & Batman, D. (2004). The Asset-Based Context Matrix: A tool for assessing children's learning opportunities and participation in natural environments. *Topics in Early Special Education, 24,* 110–120.

Winton, P., (1996). Family-professional partnerships and integrated services. In R.A. McWilliam, (Ed.), *Rethinking pull-out services in early intervention: A professional resource* (pp. 49–69). Baltimore, MD: Brookes.

Wolery, M. (2000). Behavioral and educational approaches to early intervention. In J.P. Shonkoff & S.J. Meisels (Eds.), *Handbook of early childhood intervention* (2nd ed., pp. 179–203). Cambridge, UK: Cambridge University Press.

Wolery, M. (2004). Using assessment information to plan intervention programs. In M. McLean, M. Wolery, & D. Bailey (Eds.), *Assessing infants and preschoolers with special needs* (3rd ed., pp. 517–544). Englewood Cliffs, NJ: Merrill/Prentice Hall.

Wolery, M. (2005). DEC recommended practices: Child-focused practices (Introduction). In S. Sandall, M.L. Hemmeter, B.J. Smith, & M.E. McLean, *DEC recommended practices: A comprehensive guide for practical application in early intervention/early childhood special education* (pp. 71–76). Missoula, MT: Division for Early Childhood.

Woods, J., & McCormick, K. (2002). Toward an integration of child- and family-centered practices in the assessment of preschool children: Welcoming the family. *Young Exceptional Children, 5*(3) 2–11.

Woods, J., Kashinath, S., & Goldstein, H. (2004). Effects of embedding caregiver-implemented teaching strategies in daily routines on children's communication outcomes. *Journal of Early Intervention, 26,* 175–193.

Wyngaarden Krauss, M. (2000). Family assessment within early intervention programs. In J.P. Shonkoff & S.J. Meisels (Eds.), *Handbook of early childhood intervention* (2nd ed., pp. 290–308). Cambridge, UK: Cambridge University Press.

INDEX

Activities. *See type of activity*
Adults, responsive, 27–29
American Academy of Pediatrics, 87
Approaches
    concerns about recommended, 60–61
    and intervention visits, 76
    and road map, 75–77, 83
Assessment
    authentic, 61–66, 67
    and beginning of planning, 85
    and community activities, 112
    as component of early intervention, 14, 15–16
    definition of, 68
    differing views about, 67
    of effectiveness of early intervention, 69
    for eligibility, 55–56, 57, 66, 68–69
    and environments, 64–65
    evaluation differentiated from, 68
    family–professional partnership role in,
        66–68, 69–71
    and family vision and goals, 57–60, 70, 71
    family's role in, 67
    focus of, 58, 66, 68
    and how to assess, 68
    and important people and particular places,
        64–65, 67, 69–71
    instruments for, 54
    interpretation of information from, 67
    participants in, 67
    policies and guidelines concerning, 68–69
    and preparing for the family–professional
        partnership, 70–71
    process of conducting, 57
    professional's role in, 59–60, 68, 70–71
    purpose of, 55–57, 68, 69–70
    questions to guide, 54, 63, 66–67
    and road map, 73
    and routine activities, 53, 54, 59, 61, 63, 67
    sources of information for, 69
    summary about, 69–71
    traditional, 60–61
    and what to assess, 68
    and when and where should the assessment
        take place, 67
Assistive technology, 76
Authentic assessment, 61–66, 67

Bernheimer, L., 98

Cabrera family
    assessment of, 52–53, 54, 56–57, 62, 67
    and everyday learning and development,
        19–20, 21, 22–23, 24, 25, 29–30, 31, 32, 33
    and important people and particular places,
        64, 65
    and strategies, 65
    transitions of, 138, 139, 140, 141
    vision of, 132
Carmina family
    assessment of, 56, 59
    and components of early intervention, 14,
        15–18
    and focus on the family and child, 37, 38, 39,
        40, 41–42, 43, 46, 47, 48
    and intervention visits, 93, 96, 97
    outcomes for, 136
    road map for, 78, 81, 82, 83, 84
    service coordination for, 117, 119, 123, 124, 128
    transitions for, 136, 137
Casual activities, 110
Checkpoints, 75
Child
    community experiences of, 111
    impact of family on, 38–40
    uniqueness of, 133
Choicemaking, 135
Coaching, 90, 113
Coles-Williams family
    road map for, 72, 73, 74, 75, 76, 77, 78, 80,
        81–82, 83, 84
    service coordination for, 117–18, 119, 122,
        123–25, 126, 128, 129
    transitions for, 137–38
    vision of, 132

177

ABOUT THE AUTHOR

Bonnie Kielty, Ed.D., is an Assistant Professor of the Child and Family Development faculty in the Department of Special Education and Child Development at the University of North Carolina, Charlotte. She has previously held faculty positions at Teachers College, Columbia University and University of Connecticut. Dr. Keilty's research focuses on early intervention practices, including home visiting, family support, and assessment. All of her work stresses the translation of research and theory to practice. Dr. Keilty received her doctorate in Early Intervention/Early Childhood Special Education from George Washington University, where she also received her Masters degree in Early Intervention and a Graduate Certificate in Maternal and Child Health. As an early interventionist, Dr. Keilty has worked in a variety of settings, including the home, community, classroom, and hospital. In addition to mentoring students and doing her research, Dr. Keilty enjoys collaborating with early intervention and other community programs to support their work on behalf of families with young children.